BOOKS BY JOHN GASPARD

The Como Lake Players Mysteries
ACTING CAN BE MURDER
DYING TO AUDITION
REHEARSED TO DEATH

The Eli Marks Mystery Series
THE AMBITIOUS CARD (#1)
THE BULLET CATCH (#2)
THE MISER'S DREAM (#3)
THE LINKING RINGS (#4)
THE FLOATING LIGHT BULB (#5)
THE ZOMBIE BALL (#6)
THE MAGIC SQUARE (#7)
THE SELF-WORKING TRICK (#8)

Stand-Alone Novels
THE SWORD & MR. STONE
A CHRISTMAS CARL
THE GREYHOUND OF THE BASKERVILLES
THE RIPPEROLOGISTS

THE SELF-WORKING TRICK (AND OTHER STORIES)

AN ELI MARKS SHORT MYSTERY COLLECTION

JOHN GASPARD

ALBERT'S BRIDGE
BOOKS

THE SELF-WORKING TRICK (and other stories)

An Eli Marks Short Mystery Collection

First Edition | January 2022

www.elimarksmysteries.com

"The Last Customer" was first published in "Blood Work," published by Down & Out Books in 2018.

CONTENTS

"It is better, of course, to know useless things than to know nothing."

— TOM STOPPARD

INTRODUCTION

The question I get asked most frequently (after, *"Excuse me, sir, are you supposed to be here?"*) is this: how does a non-magician write convincingly about the life of a working magician and his cohorts?

Before I started the Eli Marks mystery series, I knew practically nothing about the art and craft of being a magician. However, I did know plenty of working magicians, probably more than my share. Which gave me a bit of a head start.

Mostly, I blame Jim Cunningham. He's the narrator of all the Eli Marks audiobooks (and the co-host of Behind the Page: The Eli Marks podcast). Many, many years ago, while working at one corporate event or another, he had this odd habit. He would drop a very small leather ball (about the size of a walnut) from one hand to the other.

Over and over and over.

"What are you doing?" I'd ask, because he'd been doing it at every event for like, a year.

"Working on a French Drop and a Retention Vanish."

"Still?"

"Yep."

Fast forward a bit and Jim mentions he'd love to star in a play about Houdini and maybe we should write it together. So, to get the ball rolling, I went to the Houdini Museum in Appleton, Wisconsin and discover two things:

1. Houdini wasn't a very nice guy, and I didn't want to spend a lot of time with him, so *No Thanks* to the play; and,

2. Hey, there's a magic convention going on in this hotel!

Here's what you need to know: There are two parts to most magic conventions. The first is a series of lectures and demonstrations, in which actual magicians walk you through how they do their tricks. My wife, Amy, wanted no part of that. But she'd brought a book and was happy hanging out with our adopted greyhound (the hotel allowed dogs) while I attended some lectures.

But the second part of the convention was the best part: They had a Gala show, in which all sorts of magicians performed. Over the course of a couple hours, I saw more magicians than I had in my entire life.

And I was intrigued.

Then, not long after, there was another magic convention, right here in town. Jim Cunningham suggested I go. So, I did, and I saw a bunch more magicians, including the *amazing* John Carney.

And I continue to be intrigued.

Around this same time, I'd been thinking about ideas for a mystery series, starring an affable hero and a cranky older mentor. (That dynamic was my favorite part of my first novel, *The Ripperologists.* You'll find early versions of Eli and Uncle Harry within its pages.)

And then it occurred to me: I know more magicians than most people. Magicians are interesting people, usually pretty smart. And a bit quirky. Plus, the names of their tricks would make great book titles: *The Ambitious Card, The Bullet Catch, The Linking Rings, The Miser's Dream* ...

And thus, Eli Marks was conceived.

But first: I had to learn to sound like a magician, at least on paper.

Enter: Suzanne The Magician. A world class magician who not only lives in the Twin Cities, but also (occasionally) offers lessons.

And so, my training began. While Suzanne was, ostensibly, teaching me the sleights and moves I'd need to perform an Ambitious Card routine, she was actually doing a whole lot more. I was learning the day-to-day concerns of a working magician. What the gigs are like, what the crowds are like, what the clients are like.

At the same time, I was reading books about magicians, like Jay Marshall and Dai Vernon and David Berglas. And devouring instructional books, like Joshua Jay's *Magic: The Complete Course* and Henry Hay's *The Amateur Magician's Handbook* and Corinda's *13 Steps to Mentalism*.

I was also listening to podcasts about magicians, in particular *The Magic Newswire*, produced by Dodd Vickers. In addition to long-form interviews with top magicians from around the world, the podcast also featured occasional round-table discussions with working magicians. For an outsider like myself, it was like sitting in a bar every week and eavesdropping on the hilarious conversation at the next table.

All of this was invaluable in launching Eli Marks with *The Ambitious Card*.

But it didn't stop there. In order to keep sounding like a magician in subsequent novels, I had to keep studying. Reading more books. Listening to more podcasts. Seeing more magic shows (probably too many magic shows).

Eight books later, it appears to have paid off. I've yet to have one magician complain that I got a trick wrong. In fact, one of the best magicians in the world, Teller (of Penn & Teller), paid me the greatest compliment in an email:

Hi, John,

I was in the exact right mood for a detective novel and enjoyed The Linking Rings.

I especially liked the accurate behind-the-scenes aspect of it. Usually, magic detective stories don't really have a clue about the mentality and preoccupations of magicians. Yours is true to life.

Love and thanks,

Teller

So that happened.

* * *

For this eighth book in the series, I wanted to try something a little bit different.

After batting around a number of possible directions, I remembered Eli's ex-wife, Deirdre, often mentioned how many times Eli had helped the police solve bizarre and difficult crimes. Those cases were alluded to, but never discussed in any great detail.

Maybe now was the time to take a deeper dive into those stories.

What follows are a dozen different Eli Marks exploits from throughout his career. Some take place right after his divorce, some take place while he and Megan are dating, and some occur after he's started to run the bar next to the magic shop.

While ten of the dozen stories are brand new, two of them have been published before.

The Invisible Assistant was the first Eli Marks short story. I'd come up with a fun murder/suicide plot years ago (on second thought, maybe *fun* isn't the right word) and realized it would be a perfect crime for Eli to solve in front of his ex-wife and her new husband. Readers seemed to like it and so I gave it away for free whenever I could, to help attract people to the full Eli Marks series.

The second short story, *The Last Customer,* came about as part of an anthology to honor one of the late owners of the Once Upon A Crime bookstore in Minneapolis. The only requirements were that the story had to take place in a bookstore and involve a tuba. I fudged a bit and added a wall of books to Chicago Magic, so it kind of became a bookstore. That particular story has had a lot of legs, becoming first a story, then an audiobook, then an animation, and finally a comic book (in both digital and hardcopy formats). Again, people seemed to like it and I gave it away for free whenever I could.

As for the rest of the stories in the book, who knows where they come from? It's not always possible to trace origins or ideas.

I'm pretty sure a prank performed by Banksy was the starting point for one story, and a gag performed on fellow magicians by David Williamson provided the seed for another. A magic trick performed in *The Miser's Dream* comes back to haunt Eli in one story, while another notion popped up while visiting a new townhome purchased by my niece.

The title story came about after a friend directed a popular suspense play at a local theater; after I started the story, I realized it could easily connect to my other series, *The Como Lake Players Mystery Series* (written under the pen name Bobbie Raymond). It was fun playing around with this one-time mash-up, but I'm not sure if Eli and the other series will cross paths again. However, as Eli says in the story, never say never.

Anyway, to the best of my recollection, that's how we got to this point: a book of Eli Marks short stories.

Thanks, as always, for your interest in the series. Eli and

Uncle Harry look forward to joining you on more adventures in the years to come.

Minneapolis
> *January 2022*
> https://www.elimarksmysteries.com/

THE INVISIBLE ASSISTANT

"Now for my next effect, I'm going to need another volunteer."

I timed my statement to land just as the applause from the last trick was starting to wane. I had gone through a well-received Ambitious Card routine with the blonde volunteer to my left *(What was her name again? Jan? Jane? Joan?)* and now I needed another willing soul to join the two of us on stage.

"You know, just to ensure that I haven't pre-arranged any of this, let's make the selection of the next volunteer more, I don't know ... random," I said casually, as if I didn't say that same phrase in the exact same way in every show.

"We'll let chance decide who is going to join the two of us here on stage," I continued, neatly side-stepping the need to remember the blonde's name. "I'm going to toss this into the crowd," I said, picking up the bowling ball I had made magically appear earlier in the act. "And whoever catches it ..."

Laughter drown out the rest of the sentence, as it always did, which was convenient as I didn't actually have an ending for that sentence. I dropped the heavy ball to the stage and reached into my bag, pulling out a bright orange Nerf ball.

"You know, after the unfortunate incident that happened at the last show, let's try this instead. Heads up!"

I tossed the Nerf ball into the center of the crowd and a hand shot up and grabbed it in mid-air. "Terrific," I said, squinting, trying to see past the bright stage lights, which were positioned low and directly in my eyes. That was often the case when doing a corporate show in a low-ceilinged hotel ballroom.

"Now toss it somewhere else in the room." The ball sailed through the air again and was snatched by another hand. "Great, now to really make it random, why don't you toss it one more time?"

The ball sailed across the room, flying over all the folks finishing their identical chicken lunches, and headed straight toward a couple who had taken a standing-room only spot on the far wall. Fortunately, the man had great timing, reaching out and snatching the ball out of the air before it could hit the woman in the face.

With the stage lights in my eyes this was all a squinty tableau, but I sensed the man wasn't enthusiastic about being the final catcher in this selection process. Coaxing would be required.

"Impressive catch, sir," I said, stepping to the edge of the stage. "Come on up and give us a hand, will you?" My Uncle Harry had taught me that particular phrasing, which was designed to get the audience to applaud without realizing that they were being asked to do so. They responded on cue and the man who had caught the last toss of the Nerf ball began to move hesitantly toward the front of the room

In my new position at the lip of the stage, I was finally able to get a look at him, as well as the woman he was standing with. Although it took me a moment longer than it should have to recognize her.

It was my ex-wife. And the guy with the great timing who

was trudging slowly toward the stage was her relatively new husband.

* * *

"AND WHAT IS YOUR NAME?" I asked as he stepped onto the stage. He glared at me because he knew damned well I knew his name. But this was a show, after all, and I had to keep things moving.

"Fred," he growled.

"Fred," I repeated with more pep than was really required. I traditionally always referred to him by his full name and title, Homicide Detective Fred Hutton, but I'd have to set that annoying habit aside for the time being. "Fred, please step to my right, and Joan—" I turned to the blonde.

"Melissa," she corrected.

"Melissa, of course, if you would stand here on my left."

I had done this routine maybe a thousand times, but the sudden surprise addition of my ex-wife's husband on-stage— not to mention my ex-wife in the audience— had scrambled the bit in my head.

"I don't know if you folks can feel it out there, but there is a real chemistry between these two volunteers," I lied. In reality, there could not have been less chemistry on stage, as witnessed by the two stiffs flanking me. I soldiered on.

"To demonstrate the connection, I propose we perform a short experiment, using some playing cards and these two powerfully attractive personalities." The flat response this elicited from both volunteers actually produced a collective chuckle from the crowd.

With that, I launched into my Cards Across routine, counting three cards into Melissa's outstretched hand, and then seven cards into the hand that Homicide Detective Fred Hutton had reluctantly put forward. I caught his eye as I finished counting the seventh card; the icy stare he gave me told me exactly how much he was enjoying his time on stage.

"To recap," I continued, doing my best to remember where I was in the routine and where I needed to go. "I have placed three cards in Melissa's hands, and seven cards in Fred's hands." I nearly used his full name and title but caught myself at the last second. "Now, with the help of my invisible assistant, we will demonstrate the powerful attraction between these two happy volunteers."

This produced another ripple of laughter. I plowed forward, using Homicide Detective Fred Hutton's stone face to great comic effect, as I completed each phase of the trick, calling on the help of the invisible assistant at each key point.

First, when he counted the cards, Homicide Detective Fred Hutton found that he had eight cards. He counted again and found that he now held nine cards. At the same time, the blonde's stack of cards diminished from three to two and then to one. The routine came to an end with all ten cards in Fred's hand, and only one card in the blonde's. That card, of course, was her selected and signed card from the earlier Ambitious Card routine.

The audience gave the performance a better response than it really deserved and for a brief moment I considered ending the show right there. But I could hear my Uncle Harry's voice in the back of my head, admonishing me for considering ending the act with volunteers still on stage. *"The final applause should be for you and you alone,"* he would have said. *"No magician worth his salt wants to share a standing ovation with a volunteer."*

Although such an ovation seemed unlikely, I ushered the two volunteers off the stage, persuading the audience to give them "another well deserved round of applause." I then moved right into the classic magical snowstorm effect which I—and virtually every other magician in the world—used as my finale when a big finish is required.

I triggered my iPod with a remote switch in my pocket and suddenly the room was filled with Nat King Cole singing *Walking in a Winter Wonderland*, as a snowstorm appeared in my hands and blew out onto the first three rows. This brought the show to a quasi-rousing close and littered the stage with small bits of white paper, which I'm sure is always a delight for the hotel cleaning staff.

The corporate meeting planner met me as I came off stage with a big grin and a check that, sadly, wasn't nearly as large as her smile.

* * *

"Imagine my surprise when I saw you two in the audience," I said.

"Imagine my surprise when you called Fred on stage," replied my ex-wife.

Homicide Detective Fred Hutton declined to contribute to our conversation, instead choosing to stare at a point somewhere in a far corner of the hotel restaurant. His wife, Deirdre, was taking more delight in his impromptu performance than I might have expected. When we were married, she kept a cool demeanor at nearly all times and rarely took delight in anything, especially me. We were considered to be, as many people later confessed, an odd match.

"That was a nice routine," she continued. "With the cards moving between the people and the invisible assistant."

"Thanks, that's *Cards Across*. A classic. Next time you're in Vegas, check out Mac King's version. It's sublime." The waitress took that moment to appear with the coffee I had ordered. I stirred in some cream and took a long sip. "Had I known you two wanted to see the show, I would have reserved you some actual seats."

"It was something of a spur of the moment decision."

This produced a barely audible grunt from Homicide Detective Fred Hutton.

"So, it wasn't a mutual decision?" I suggested.

"Maybe not, but here we are," Deirdre said, leaning forward, clearly finished with the chitchat portion of the meeting. "I want to get your take on something, a case we're working on."

While we were married, Deirdre had risen steadily through the District Attorney's office and was now well ensconced, and well respected, as an assistant DA. Her close working relationship with the Minneapolis Police Department's Homicide division had produced several stunning murder convictions and one divorce.

"You've read about the Josiah Manning murder-suicide?" she asked.

I nodded and took another sip of coffee. "I heard about it in passing," I said. "But I don't know any of the details."

"But you know who Josiah Manning was?"

I shrugged. "He was a big anti-death penalty, anti-suicide guy, right?"

"The biggest."

"And he killed someone in the opposition?"

"Not just someone. He basically killed the opposition. Harley Keller, the leader of what people had come to call the pro-death movement."

"Because he believed in suicide?"

"More than believed. Harley Keller was a true zealot. He was the suicide poster child."

"They have that? Weird." Although my alleged quip drew only a scowl from Deirdre, I thought I detected the faintest hint of a smile on Homicide Detective Fred Hutton's lips. Then it was gone, as quickly as it had appeared.

"So, let me get this straight: The anti-suicide guy who

believed fervently in the sanctity of life, murdered the pro-suicide guy and then to top it all off, he killed himself?"

"That's what the police believe," Deirdre said, throwing a sidelong glance at her husband. He did not return it.

"Well, get Alanis Morissette on the line, because that's pretty ironic."

Deirdre sighed. "Eli, do you have any cultural references that are less than twenty years old?"

I was tempted to dazzle her with a Nipsey Russell-style poem on the topic but thought better of it. "So, your opinion differs from that of the Homicide department?"

"On several key points, yes," she said as she began to dig through her purse. "Which is why I wanted to talk to you. Why I wanted both of us to talk to you," she added. "On occasion you've offered a unique perspective that I think could be useful in this instance."

"I believe the phrase you used when we were married was, 'You have a bizarre way of looking at things.'"

"Yes," she said, leaving it at that. She pulled an iPad from the depths of her purse. "I want you to look at this," she said, clicking and swiping until she'd found what she was looking for. "This is about four years old and is just one of many, many similar videos." She hit a play button and handed me the iPad.

I tilted it, so that Homicide Detective Fred Hutton could see as well, but he waved me away.

"I've seen it," he said, crossing his arms and slouching back into his chair, setting his gaze once again on an invisible point across the room.

The sound of an argument pulled my attention back to the iPad. Actually, it wasn't technically an argument, as only one person was talking. Or, more accurately, shouting.

"That's Harley Keller," Deirdre pointed out as I looked at the man on the screen.

He was gaunt and pale, a crew cut consisting of wisps of white hair covering his large, boney head. His eyes, which burned at someone off-camera, were a sharp, steely blue. He was shouting—ranting, really—so vehemently that small specks of white spittle were visible around his lips and on his chin.

The video cut at that point to another man who listened intently to the bile being thrown at him. Like Harley, he appeared to be in his early sixties, but there was a calmness and warmth to him that made him seem younger.

"Josiah Manning?" I suggested, beating Deirdre to the punch. She nodded and I turned back to the screen.

"Death is a basic human right," Harley was shouting. "A person has a right to their death just as they have a right to their life. If I wish to end my life, that is my personal decision, and you and the public and the state have no right to stand in the way of my decision." He stared daggers at Josiah, seeming to dare him to speak.

Josiah returned the stare, but his was warm and without judgment.

"Don't you want to answer that?" Harley snapped.

"Gladly," Josiah said softly. "It's just that, since you have interrupted me at every opportunity this evening, I just wanted to make sure that I in turn was not about to—inadvertently—interrupt you."

Harley sat back and spread his hands open before him, giving the floor to Josiah.

"While I certainly respect your opinion," he said quietly. "I cannot endorse it nor justify it. Life, in all of its forms, is sacred. It was given to us and it is not ours to take away, whether via a lethal injection in a prison or an exhaust hose in a garage—"

"So, you insist," Harley said, cutting him off, "That you have a right to keep me alive and I don't have a right to choose the time of my death? Is that what you're saying? But that is complete and utter—"

Some network censor somewhere had pulled the sound down for the next few profanity-laden seconds of his rant, so Deirdre took that opportunity to take the iPad back and hit the Pause button.

"Wow," I said. "After seeing that, if you told me one of those guys killed the other guy and then himself, I would have sworn it was Harley Keller who pulled that trigger twice. Not Josiah Manning."

"My point exactly," Deirdre said as she slipped the tablet back into the dark recesses of her purse. "I'm just having a bit of trouble getting the Homicide department to see things my way."

"It's cut and dried," Homicide Detective Fred Hutton grumbled. "And that's the truth."

"The truth is rarely cut and never dried," I mis-quoted, not at all sure what that was supposed to mean. "So, what does Homicide think happened?"

"Harley Keller invited Josiah Manning to his home," he began.

"His home?"

"Harley Keller lived in a townhouse on Cedar Lake," Deirdre explained.

Homicide Detective Fred Hutton gave her a long look and then continued. "Harley Keller invited Josiah Manning to his home," he repeated slowly. "At some point the two must have gone upstairs to Mr. Keller's office on the second floor. While in that office, Josiah Manning shot Harley Keller point blank in the chest."

"Yikes," I said involuntarily.

"He died almost immediately," Homicide Detective Fred Hutton continued, ignoring my short outburst. "Josiah Manning then went downstairs, sat down in a chair in the living room, put the gun in his mouth and pulled the trigger."

"Where did you find the gun?"

"On the floor next to the chair."

"Powder burns?"

"Residue was found on the fingers of Josiah Manning's right hand."

"How about Harley Keller?"

"His hands were clean."

I sat back and considered what I had heard. I took a sip of my coffee, which had already turned cold. "Maybe someone else shot them both and then left?"

Homicide Detective Fred Hutton shook his head. "The place was locked up tight. Both front and rear entrances were fortified with heavy chain security locks. All windows locked. From the inside. Responding officers had to break down the front door after neighbors reported gunshots."

"Suicide note?"

He shook his head.

I took another sip of coffee and turned to Deirdre. "And you think it happened some other way?"

"Yes," she said.

"What's odd about this," I said as a new thought began to dawn on me, "Is that in reality there were three deaths that night." This produced curious looks from both of them.

"How do you figure?" Deirdre asked.

I counted them out on my fingers for emphasis. "Harley Keller and Josiah Manning both died, "I said. "But so too did Josiah Manning's reputation. I mean, the method of his death will now always overshadow his life's work. The anti-suicide guy will now always be known as the guy who killed himself. And Harley Keller certainly had the motive to put that reputation to rest." I finished the rest of my coffee. "Can we go look at the crime scene?" I said as I stood up.

Deirdre was already on her feet.

"I thought you'd never ask."

* * *

You know how you can sometimes tell when a couple is arguing, even when you can't hear them? I mean, just by their body language? That's the sense I got as I followed the happy couple across town to the Cedar Lake neighborhood. From my vantage point in the front seat of my car, I could see them talking in the front seat of theirs. And from where I sat, it did not look like a happy conversation.

For some odd reason, that made me sad. Because, I figured, if she had to leave me, the very least she could do would try to be happy with the guy she left me for. I mean, otherwise, what was the point?

Harley Keller lived—or had lived—in a townhouse on Cedar Lake. It's the most mysterious of the Minneapolis chain of lakes, primarily because it was impossible to drive around it. You could drive past it, but not around it.

His townhouse, like all the others connected to it, looked relatively new and completely identical. A different, brightly colored windsock hung in front of each entryway, probably in a failed attempt to aid in the identification process.

Deirdre and Homicide Detective Fred Hutton were already unlocking the front door when I caught up to them. "No crime scene tape?" I observed.

"It's no longer a crime scene," Homicide Detective Fred Hutton grunted as he pushed the door open. I was surprised to be greeted by the sound of a yipping dog.

"Hey, there's a dog," I said, clearly stating the obvious. "That's weird. Why is there a dog?"

"There are a variety of pets still in residence," Homicide Detective Fred Hutton stated flatly.

I looked to Deirdre for a more complete explanation.

"Harley Keller had a dog, three cats, a bird and an aquarium. We were going to turn them all over to animal control, but the next of kin requested against that," she said. "The lady next door stops in several times a day to take care of them. His next of kin are coming to town at the end of the week to handle the estate."

"That's quite a menagerie," I said. "I mean, for a pro-death kind of guy like Harley Keller."

"Yes, it is," Homicide Detective Fred Hutton said with what sounded like a sigh. This was followed immediately by something that sounded like a sneeze. And then another. And another.

"Fred's allergic to cats. And dogs," Deirdre said by way of explanation.

At that moment a small mutt of a dog came racing towards us, yelping happily. Because Homicide Detective Fred Hutton was the only one of us allergic to animals, the dog naturally went right for him. He dropped a slimy, spit-covered rubber ball at the detective's feet. Homicide Detective Fred Hutton gave the ball a disgruntled kick as he pulled out a handkerchief to catch his next sneeze. The handkerchief arrived a millisecond too late.

As the dog chased after the errant ball, a large tabby cat arrived and began to wend its way around Homicide Detective Fred Hutton's ankles. This cat was soon joined by another cat, this one small and black. Then the dog returned with the ball and the next phase of sneezing began.

"Can we proceed?" Homicide Detective Fred Hutton pleaded between sneezes.

"By all means," I agreed. "Give me the nickel tour."

"Sure. The dog is named Gypsy and the cats are Jinx, Penny and—" Deirdre was cut off before she could complete her list.

"He means a tour of the crime scene," Homicide Detective Fred Hutton barked.

Oh," she said, acting innocent. "I thought it wasn't a crime scene anymore."

I put up a hand to stop them. "The way you two are behaving, it feels like it could easily become a crime scene again, at any moment. Could we just stick to the facts of the case?"

While her husband blew his nose, Deirdre pointed out the chair where Josiah Manning had—allegedly—shot himself. It was an oversized recliner, upholstered in a light blue plush fabric. A large bloodstain covered the chair's headrest. On a hunch, I tugged on each armrest. They opened, revealing a storage chamber within each arm. Both chambers were not only empty but spotless.

Deirdre pointed out the place on the floor where he had dropped the gun. I gestured toward the chair and she nodded her permission. I slowly sat in the recliner, taking care not to lean back on the headrest. The blood had long since dried, but human nature dictated that I keep my distance, so I did. I mimed the motions of putting a gun in my mouth and pulling the trigger. My arm dropped to the side. I looked down to see if my imaginary gun had landed in the spot Deirdre had indicated. To my mind's eye, it was a direct hit.

She then headed toward the stairway. I followed her and, once he was able to disentangle himself from his animal friends, Homicide Detective Fred Hutton trailed behind us. We passed an impressively huge fish tank built into one wall. The fish swam aimlessly back and forth, looking exotic and colorful. I glanced at the tank and then back to the sniffling mess behind me.

"You allergic to fish too?" I asked, trying to hide how much I was enjoying the question.

"With my luck, yes," he said as another sneeze arrived. We followed Deirdre up the stairs, with both cats doing their best to get under Homicide Detective Fred Hutton's feet as he blearily navigated the stairs.

Harley Keller's office was a large room at the top of the staircase. A computer sat atop an IKEA-style desk, with matching bookcases lining one wall. Photos of Harley with notables lined the other wall. The rest of the room consisted of a series of cat beds, a dog bed, and various carpeted structures designed to provide an indoor cat with the climbing experience they were being denied by being forced to live inside. To prove that thesis, a cat I hadn't yet seen was resting atop the highest structure in the room.

Homicide Detective Fred Hutton stood in the doorway and sneezed. As if responding to this call, Gypsy had returned and dropped his spit-covered ball at the detective's feet. Once he realized the human had no desire to play with him, the dog sniffed at the ball and then marched over to his rag-filled dog bed, circling the bed three times before finally settling in.

I looked down at a large, dark brown bloodstain in the center of the room, which had soaked into the cream-colored plush carpeting.

"Based on the position of the body and the blood splatter, it appears that Harley was shot right here," Deirdre said, pointing to where the body had fallen.

"So," I said, trying to work out the chronology. "Harley and Josiah came up here. Josiah shoots Harley in the chest. He falls there," I said, indicating the bloodstain. "Josiah then marches downstairs and shoots himself in the head."

"That's the police version, yes," she said.

I stooped down. From where I was standing, I could see down the stairs into the living room. However, the recliner where Josiah had shot himself was not in view. I turned to Deirdre. "And what's your theory? That Harley shot Josiah and then shot himself?"

"That makes more sense to me."

"Even though the facts clearly do not support that supposition?" Homicide Detective Fred Hutton's voice was a little ragged from the sneezing, but his attitude came through loud and clear.

"I think if you insist on looking at only <u>some</u> of the facts, you can easily reach the wrong conclusion."

I recognized Deirdre's tone and my stomach tightened in what can only be called a Pavlovian response. I crossed the room and sat at the desk, trying to gather my thoughts while the happy couple continued to squabble. I did my best to block out their bickering while I sorted through the elements of the puzzle.

I knew from past experience that if Deirdre was insisting about a point this vehemently, there was likely something behind it and it was worth pursuing. She was adamant that something wasn't quite right in what we were seeing. She didn't believe that Josiah shot Harley and then himself. And, given what little I knew about the two men, I was inclined to agree.

However, if Harley merely wanted Josiah dead, he could have just shot him and then, if he was so inclined, he could have shot himself. But instead, he felt the need to kill Josiah's reputation as well. But how?

I thought about all the methods I knew to get an object from one side of the stage to the other. All the ways I had learned to take something off a person without them knowing it. And the more useful art of putting something on them without tipping them off.

I thought about mirrors and stooges and dual realities and other forms of misdirection. I thought about my act from that afternoon. And then a glimmer of an idea began to take hold in the back of my head. But it was having trouble making itself heard above the din in the room.

"Could you two please knock it off?" I finally said, saying it much louder than I had intended. My volume and tone produced the desired effect and they both stopped in mid-argument. "I can't hear myself think," I added at a much lower level. I got up and saw that they were each looking at me like contrite children.

I moved to the center of the room. "So, this is where Harley was standing when he was shot?"

Deirdre nodded, double-checked it with Homicide Detective Fred Hutton, and then nodded again.

"Is it possible that someone could use a handgun like the one used in this case and shoot themselves in the chest? I mean, hold their arm out, point the gun at their own chest and shoot themselves?" I demonstrated what I meant, stretching out my arm and turning my hand back toward my chest.

Deirdre started to answer, but Homicide Detective Fred Hutton beat her to it. "Yes, but a bullet to the heart would produce nearly instant death," he said. "There would be no time to get the gun downstairs. Not to mention the powder burns on the hand," he added.

Deirdre held up a hand for him to stop talking. He didn't look like he wanted to, but a sudden sneeze shifted his attention away from me and back to his handkerchief.

Deirdre jumped on this pause. "What are you thinking?" she said, stepping toward me.

"What if it happened this way," I began, heading toward the door. "Oh, do either of you have a gun? I mean, an unloaded gun, about the same size that was used here?"

Still unable to speak, Homicide Detective Fred Hutton shook his head and then registered a look of surprise as Deirdre began to dig through her purse. A moment later, she produced a small handgun. "I checked it out of the armory this morning," she said by way of explanation. "In case we needed to re-enact anything. Don't worry, it's not loaded."

"Great," I said, taking the gun from her, surprised at its heft. It was a little heavy, but not too heavy for what I had in mind. "Also, do you have any gloves, like the ones you use when sifting through evidence?"

Deirdre nodded at Homicide Detective Fred Hutton, who glared back at her. There was a short, tense standoff, and then he acquiesced. He put his handkerchief in one pocket and then pulled a pair of thin, latex gloves out of the other. He handed them to me, and I pulled one onto my right hand as I sprinted out of the room and down the stairs. I ducked into the kitchen for a moment. The couple had made it to the base of the stairs by the time I returned.

"Okay," I said, beginning my impromptu presentation. "Let's try this scenario on for size. I am Harley Keller and I have invited Josiah Manning over to my townhouse. I'm not entirely sure how I got him here, maybe something about burying the hatchet, but anyway, I invite him and he comes over."

I walked to the front door and mimed each action as I narrated. "Josiah comes in the front door. I welcome him and lock the door behind him and chain the door. Then, with his back to me, I knock him out with the butt of the gun."

I went through these actions, pretending to strike and then lower an unconscious body into the recliner. "Now, this puts a pretty big wound on the back of Josiah's head, but that will be obliterated when I put the gun in his mouth, wrap his finger around the trigger and then pull it. Blam!"

My impression of the sound of the gun was loud enough to make Deirdre jump. I patted her on the shoulder as I headed back to the stairs. "Sorry about that," I said. "Anyway, now Josiah is dead, and he's got powder marks on his right hand. The first half of my plan is completed. Now for phase two."

I took the stairs two at a time, and then had to wait while the couple trudged back up the stairs. Once again, the cats did their best to trip their new friend up. I waited patiently for them to arrive and then waited a few more seconds for another quick round of sneezing.

"Okay, so now it's Harley's turn," I said, stretching my right arm as far in front of me as I could and pointing the gun back toward my chest. "I shoot myself point blank in the heart, drop the gun and die a few seconds later." I looked up and smiled at the couple in the doorway. "Just that simple," I added.

Deirdre squinted at me and Homicide Detective Fred Hutton shook his head.

"Now," I continued, "you're probably wondering how Harley got the gun from the floor next to him, down the stairs and next to Josiah's body?"

"Yes, we are," Deirdre said, sounding annoyed. "That's the whole point."

"Well, I think he did it the same way I got the cards from Joan's hands to his hands during my act today," I said, gesturing toward Homicide Detective Fred Hutton.

"Melissa," he said and then blew his nose.

"What?"

"The volunteer's name was Melissa."

"Whatever."

"So," Deirdre said, clearly frustrated, 'How did you get the cards from her hands to his hands?"

I smiled. "With an invisible assistant," I said. Before she could pursue this further, I checked that I was standing in the right spot and pointed the gun at my chest.

"Blam!" I shouted, again making her jump. I clutched my chest with one hand, while dropping the gun to the floor with the other. And then I prayed.

A moment later my prayers were rewarded as we heard the patter of paws on carpet. We turned to see that Gypsy had jumped out of his dog bed and was scampering across the room. He happily picked up the gun between his teeth—it was a mouthful, but he was able to grasp it tightly—and then he trotted out of the room and down the stairs. We followed, heading halfway down the stairs, just in time to see him drop the gun right next to the recliner. He started back toward us, forcing me to run back up the stairs to Harley's office.

"A dog that smart, you could teach him that trick in just a few days," I said over my shoulder.

"Well, that covers the gun," Homicide Detective Fred Hutton said between sneezes. "But what about the powder burns?"

I returned to my position in the center of the office and peeled off the glove. "In the few moments I have left after shooting myself," I explained, "I peel off the glove and drop it to the floor." I did just that.

"But we would have found it by the body," Homicide Detective Fred Hutton began. But he was interrupted by Gypsy, who ran back into the room and up to the glove. He sniffed it for a brief second, then picked it up and carried it back to his dog bed, where he began to chew on it happily. In just a few seconds it was virtually shredded.

"I ducked into the kitchen and put a dog treat into that glove," I said. "But I suspect that Harley probably used a linen glove and soaked it in chicken or beef broth the day before. I think a thorough examination of Gypsy's dog bed might even produce a few remaining tatters of that glove, which would undoubtedly still have powder burns on it."

Homicide Detective Fred Hutton made a move toward the bed and the glove Gypsy was currently enjoying, but the dog growled and bared his teeth. The detective wisely stepped back from the dog bed.

"We'll look into that," he said dryly.

"What I'm really hoping, Detective, is that you can see it in your heart to not arrest that dog as an accessory to murder." This produced a smile and a chuckle. But not from Homicide Detective Fred Hutton. He turned and spoke sharply to Deirdre.

"That's not funny."

"Oh, I don't know," she said. "It's a little funny. You just have no sense of humor."

This remark triggered a new phase of their ongoing argument. I listened for a few, painful seconds, and then held up my hands in protest.

"Here's the thing," I said as I backed toward the door. "I am happy to help you out from time to time, but if it means having to endure an episode of *"The Bickersons"* every time I see you two, count me out." Deirdre gave me a puzzled look. "In case you're keeping track, that reference is probably well over sixty years old." This did little to abate her confusion.

"Thanks again, Gypsy, for being the best invisible assistant I've never seen," I continued, tossing a remaining dog treat across the room. The little dog jumped up and caught it in the air.

As I headed down the stairs, I could hear the crunching of that dog treat, followed by the sound of an argument beginning anew. This was cut short by another flurry of sneezing, which was the last sound I heard before I shut the door behind me.

THE TRICK THAT CANNOT BE EXPLAINED

I know a trick.

That statement may seem self-evident, since I make my living—such as it is—as a magician.

What I meant to say is, I know a trick that helps me do my job. Particularly when I need to walk up to a group of strangers in a social situation and ask them if they'd like to see some magic. Experience has taught me this sort of sudden intrusion is occasionally unwelcome or, at the very least, unexpected.

When I need to accomplish this interruption at a corporate event—a walk-around gig at a company function of some kind —I find dropping a key name is the quickest entry point to granting me instant access to virtually any small group.

The name I say changes from company to company, but generally all I need to do is mention the name of the CEO—or the highest-ranking person at the event—and I am welcomed in with open arms.

"Excuse me," I might say to a small cluster of workers. "Gretchen asked me to show you a little magic tonight. Mind if I do?"

Or it might be, "Pardon me, but Dave wanted me to demonstrate something for you. Do you have a second?"

There's a lot of power in a person's first name, particularly when that person is in charge. They hear that name and, bingo, I'm in.

This ploy works equally well at wedding receptions, as I move from table to table during dinner. "Excuse me, but Susan and Mark wanted me to show you something. Do you mind if I interrupt?"

Or, "Pardon me, but Mitch and Brian asked me to stop by and entertain you folks for just a few moments..."

And I'm off and running.

I was reviewing the high success rate of my approach as I stood in the basement of this unfamiliar church. Workers were setting out food on the buffet counters and other volunteers were making the final adjustments to the small centerpieces on each of the tables that filled the low-ceilinged room.

The question which was bugging me was this: My approach certainly worked for corporate events. And it worked for weddings.

Would it also work at a *funeral*?

I was about to find out.

* * *

THE CALL HAD, at first, seemed like any other gig request: Could I perform walk-around magic at an upcoming reception?

It was only while gathering further information (the time, the place, the type of gathering) that I realized I was stepping into uncharted territory.

My agent, who has raised cluelessness to a high art, seemed unfazed as she rattled off the particulars.

"So, it's this Saturday, at Our Lady of the Immaculate Conception church in St. Paul. The funeral is at 11:00 and the lunch and reception will start about noon," Elaine said, clearly reading from what were probably hastily scribbled notes.

"Whoa, whoa, back up a second." I was holding the tip of my pen inches above my own notes, not sure I had heard the details clearly. "Did you say the *funeral* starts at 11:00?"

I could hear her through the phone, flipping through notes. "That's what I've got," she finally said. "Why, is that a weird time for a funeral to start? I'm not Catholic."

"Neither am I," I said. "But it's not the time that's grabbed my attention. Did you say I'm doing walk-around magic at a *funeral*?"

"Well, no, not at the funeral. At the reception after. Doing it at a funeral might be, I don't know, weird."

"Oh, you think so?"

I was forming the words to tell her I wasn't interested in the gig, when I glanced down at the calendar page in front of me. I had a corporate walk-around event penciled in for two weeks from now, but the client had suggested I "use a light pencil." I wasn't holding out hope for that one. Other than this possibly disappearing gig, the month was looking pretty sparse, workwise.

"Are you available?" Elaine said, sounding more distracted than usual. I could tell her mind was moving onto other clients and other matters.

"Sure, sure," I said. "I'll need a phone call with the client ahead of time, though. To work out the details."

"No problem," Elaine said. "I'll lock it down and text you the deets."

True to her word, my phone buzzed about ten minutes later with the details of the gig and the name and phone number of the client.

* * *

"*How are you all doing? Sorry to interrupt, but Sue asked me to stop by and show you one of Neville's favorite card tricks.*"

I ran that sentence over in my mind a couple of times, then tried saying it aloud—quietly—to determine if there might be any clunky consonant clusters I could trip over. It seemed fine, in principle. Although it really wasn't my introduction I was concerned with.

As it turns out, it was the trick itself which was giving me heart palpitations.

I had called the client after I spoke to my agent. She was a pleasant, if preoccupied, older woman named Sue. Her distraction seemed perfectly reasonable, as she was planning the details of her husband, Neville's, funeral.

And I was one of those details.

The conversation was short and direct: In order to help bring out her husband's personality at the event, she wanted me to walk around and perform Neville's favorite card trick.

It wasn't until she named the trick that I recognized the problem.

"He called it *The Trick You Can't Explain*," she said. Her tone suggested she wasn't one hundred percent certain she'd gotten the name right. She hadn't, but she was close. "Do you know it?"

I said that I did, which was the truth. Had she gone one step further and asked if I knew how to perform it, I would have been hard pressed to provide a fully honest response.

Describing the trick would have been equally difficult.

It had come by its title for a reason. It really could not be explained.

* * *

"*Oh, my goodness*," my uncle Harry said with a chuckle. "*The Trick That Cannot Be Explained*, you say? Well, you certainly have put your foot in it, haven't you?" This was followed by another unhelpful chortle.

"You can either spend the afternoon laughing at me or instead offer some helpful advice," I said, snapping a bit more than intended.

"There's nothing saying I can't do both," Harry replied, then held up a hand to silence any response on my part. "Calm yourself, Eli. Not to worry. I can talk you through it. That is, up to a point."

He gestured toward an empty chair at his table. He was seated in a back corner of the bar next to our magic store, Chicago Magic. The store, like the bar, was empty on this cloudy, almost rainy Wednesday afternoon. I was three days away from the funeral reception and really beginning to regret I had agreed to the gig.

"Dai Vernon gave the trick that name because it's never really the same trick twice," Harry began. He was shifting into lecture mode, so I settled myself back in my chair. "It's sort of the magical equivalent of jazz, really."

"Okay, so what's the structure?" I was feeling I might need to take some notes and did a quick search of my pockets. No paper, which was fine, because I also had no pen.

"Well, I'd say there's a beginning, middle and an end, but that isn't always the case. It could be the reverse. The middle can be the end. It might never get past the beginning. Or, when the end appears, it isn't where you thought you were headed. That's the beauty of the trick."

"And what is the trick?"

"In its simplest form, the trick is what happens and what you make of what's happened. You need to be totally in the moment, while simultaneously looking back. And forward."

"Looking back at what?"

"At what's happened so far," he said with a sly grin. "And

also at everything you've ever learned about magic. Specifically, but not always, card magic."

"You're beginning to sound like a crazed Zen master. Or a drunken Yoda."

"Again, that's why Vernon named it the way he did. It's less about moves and sleights—although those are vital to your success—and more about being in the moment and open to all possibilities. The trick, in its purest form, will be different every time."

"So, the guy whose funeral this is, Neville, he must have been a pretty good magician if this was his favorite trick?"

Harry nodded slowly. "It's certainly not for the beginner, but it's also not for the faint of heart. I know plenty of top-notch magicians who wouldn't perform it on a bet."

"Why?"

"Well, I wouldn't say it depends on luck, because I've always believed that, with the right mindset, you can make your own luck. But the simple fact is, it doesn't work all the time. That is to say, a good magician can always produce a result, but it won't necessarily be a miracle. But when it works, whoa Nellie, stand back. Because it can be spectacular. Let me demonstrate. Do you have a deck of cards? Better yet, two decks?"

While I may not consistently have paper or pen on my person, I always carry a couple standard decks with me.

I handed the cards to Harry and the lesson began.

Just as Alice stepped through the looking glass into a puzzling new imaginative world, over the next two hours Harry guided me through the byzantine maze which was *The Trick That Cannot Be Explained*. While I recognized versions of some of the effects he produced, I also witnessed miracles I couldn't explain. The results were sometimes mind-blowing, sometimes merely interesting, but every time the process—and the result —were not only different but seemingly casual. Unrehearsed. Unplanned. Often unfathomable.

It might be that all four aces appeared at once at the top of the deck. Or that your volunteer suddenly dealt out a winning hand of poker. Or that the match to a card thought of by your helper appeared within the seemingly empty card box on the table.

The number of outcomes appeared to be limited only by my imagination and skill.

Limitations with which I was intimately familiar.

Which was why the trick absolutely terrified me.

* * *

ALTHOUGH I WASN'T SCHEDULED to work until noon, I showed up an hour earlier, so I could be there for the funeral as well. It was partly out of respect, but also because I wanted to get the lay of the land. And to get a sense of the man whose favorite trick I was about to perform multiple times.

I made a quick check of the reception area in the church's basement, which was still in the process of being set up. Then I went back upstairs to find a seat, which was a trick unto itself. The place was packed. I finally was able to squeeze into a pew about a third of the way back and on the side. Then I settled in for the funeral.

By the end of the service, I felt like the biggest waste of space on this planet.

Neville sounded amazing. Big-hearted, funny, the go-to guy in a crisis, your best friend, your wisest critic; Neville was extolled by speaker after speaker during the hour-long service. From non-profit boards to overseeing pet adoptions to speaking on climate issues to Bridge, Backgammon and Scrabble clubs. Neville did it all. I couldn't see how he'd had any extra time to become a master magician, but then that was just who Neville was.

He wasn't just lauded; he was loved. The same sentiments

kept surfacing through all the remarks, but one guy—a friend from high school—seemed to say it best: "The thing about Neville was that you always came away from every encounter with him feeling you had been given a gift of some kind. I don't know how he did that." There was a murmur of agreement from the large crowd, and then the old friend went on to recount yet another of the seemingly endless acts of kindness Neville had bestowed.

Any pressure I had felt about doing justice to his favorite trick rose exponentially as the service went on. Someone who was that amazing clearly deserved a top-notch performance.

And I really wasn't convinced I was the guy to deliver it.

Make no mistake: I've bombed before, plenty of times. But the idea of bombing at a funeral really offered its own tragic implications.

To sum up: I wasn't in a good place. My only consolation was that my current situation, such as it was, was just slightly more positive than the guest of honor. But not by much.

* * *

I FOLLOWED the large crowd as they filed out of the sanctuary and down the narrow steps to the basement reception hall. As I entered the low-ceilinged room, I was delighted to discover that —with the exception of the several food-laden buffet tables— the room was filled wall-to-wall with tabletops. While there was a little standing room around the sides, the layout was designed to force people to grab some food and sit down. I doubt it had been devised with my needs in mind, but I was nonetheless happy with the outcome.

The thing about the trick—or actually the series of card tricks—I was about to perform, was that I pretty much had to do it at a table. Either I could be seated, or my spectators could be seated, or we all could be seated. But it wasn't something I could do with any great flexibility if I were standing and they were clustered around me, holding drinks or small plates of appetizers.

I stood there for a long moment as the rest of the crowd oozed in around me. In a normal walk-around situation I would've dived right in, finding a small group and starting to perform. Something, anything, that would quickly grab the attention of an intimate bunch of attendees.

But that wasn't going to happen here. I had to wait for people to go through the buffet line, get some food and then sit down. Which meant, basically, I had more time to think and more time to worry and more time to squirm.

Finally, one of the tables filled up and I stepped forward. I was feeling like an amateur skydiver about to jump for the first time; I was not at all certain I had packed my parachute properly. I took a deep breath, approached the table and jumped in headfirst.

"Sorry to interrupt, but Sue asked me to go around and perform Neville's favorite magic trick for folks. Would you like to see it?"

They agreed to the proposition and I was off and running.

And I kept running for the next hour. From table to table, one right after the other. There was no need to re-set when I'd finished at one table; I'd just grab the cards and move onto the next group.

The time sailed by like a slow-motion blur. And, boy, did I work. In order to pull off *The Trick That Cannot Be Explained*, I had to be completely present and in the moment. Every single moment.

And the truly amazing thing was, it was paying off.

It's like the stars had aligned in my favor. I'd get to a new table, set up a new situation (pick a card, think of a card, give me a number between one and twenty—I never knew until I said it just what the set-up might be). And moments later I'd floor them with a trick which used that information to great effect.

It was weird. *Really* weird.

And understand this: I don't believe in ghosts. I don't believe in unseen hands from the beyond reaching down and orchestrating events. But I couldn't deny what was happening. I was doing Neville's favorite trick—*The Trick That Cannot Be Explained*—at his funeral and it was working virtually every time.

Was I in the midst of some actual, true, paranormal experience? Were all my years of debunking coming back to literally haunt me? Was this some sort of cosmic comeuppance? The universe shaking a finger at me, saying "Hey, remember everything you thought you knew? Well buddy, think again."

Was that what was happening?

To say I was spooked might be an understatement. I tried to reassure myself by imagining what Uncle Harry would be saying in this situation: *"You make your own luck, Eli. That's all this is. This is not supernatural. This is not the ghost of Neville, reaching out to you from the beyond, guiding your hand, stacking the deck, and making things—amazing things—happen. This is just you, a good magician with solid skills, who has learned the difficult art of how to take advantage of a situation and make miracles out of it."*

I wanted to believe that. I wanted to believe I was just that good.

Of course, I knew I wasn't.

I mean, I'm pretty good. I'm better than the average guy off the street. But this level? This number of miracles one after another? I was supposed to actually believe that, somehow, I was doing that?

That seemed, at best, unlikely. To say I was feeling mixed emotions would be an understatement.

I moved steadily and methodically from table to table,

each time introducing myself with the same preplanned introduction ("Sorry to disturb you, but Sue asked me to perform
Neville's favorite card trick for you"), never really knowing
what I was going to do after that sentence. Yet somehow I
always seem to know. Every time, the next sentence came to
me. It was never the same sentence, I was always entirely in
the moment. And amazing things happened, one after
another.

I began to feel like the bishop in the movie *Caddyshack*, who
in the midst of a tremendous rainy downpour, hits amazing golf
shots, again and again. At one point he says something like,
"I'm having the greatest game of my life!" And then he misses a
shot and swears to the heavens. A moment later, he's struck
down by a bolt of lightning.

I was waiting for that moment to happen to me. When
would lightning strike me down?

* * *

THE TABLES for the reception were arranged in a large circle,
with another circle of tables within that circle. In the center
was a lone table, which was reserved for the widow, where she
was seated with what appeared to be close friends and relatives.

I had started the gig on the large, outer circle, then moved
to the smaller inner circle. My last table was literally the last
table in the center of the room.

I introduced myself to Sue, offering condolences and
thanking her for the chance to perform Neville's favorite trick
one last time.

"Oh, thank you, Eli," Sue said, smiling broadly. She was a
tiny woman with beautiful stark white hair. She grabbed my
hand and squeezed it. "Neville would have been so pleased."

"It's been my honor," I said, and I really meant it. This had
been a day like no other.

"Do the trick for us," someone said from the other side of the table. I looked down at Sue and she nodded.

"I would love to see it again," she said quietly.

So, I launched into the unknown one final time.

Was it the best version that afternoon? Maybe not, but it was darned good. I used two volunteers: one had chosen a card which had appeared, with a simple cut, in the middle of the deck, while the other's card was found all by itself in the empty card box.

The table applauded at the conclusion and I looked down at Sue, who was smiling up at me.

"Oh, Eli, that was wonderful," she said. "But that's not Neville's trick."

I was sure I hadn't heard her correctly. "Excuse me?"

"That's not Neville's trick," she repeated.

"Yes, I know. It's different every time," I began, but Sue cut me off.

"No, it was always the same. Always exactly the same." She turned to an older gentleman on her right. "George, you know how the trick goes, don't you?"

"I should say I do," he said with a grim chuckle. "Neville did it every chance he got. I must have seen it a thousand times."

He put his hand out and I surrendered the cards, not sure what I had done wrong or where this was headed. George quickly counted out a few cards and then spread the small packet, face up, for a guest across the table.

"Irene, I want you to pick one of these cards. Don't tell me what you've picked, though. Have you picked one?"

The woman nodded and George began to deal out the cards.

Into three piles. Of seven cards each. All face up.

I'm sure my expression must have reflected, at least to a degree, the turmoil I was suddenly feeling. This guy was doing *The Twenty-One Card Trick*, the simplest, most common trick on the planet. It was the go-to routine for virtually any layperson who insisted on performing a trick for me after learning I was a magician.

<u>This</u> was Neville's favorite trick?

"I'm sorry," I said as I looked down at Sue. I'm sure my utter confusion was evident in my voice. "I thought Neville's favorite trick was *The Trick That Cannot Be Explained*?"

"Oh, it was," she agreed, nodding along. "Any time I'd ask him how it was done, Neville always said the same thing: 'Honey, it's complicated, it's a math thing. It's one of those tricks I just can't explain.' So that's what we always called it. *The Trick I Can't Explain*."

I was suddenly hit with a hard punch of clarity right to the face. I must have misheard her on the phone. Had I asked a follow-up question—*any* follow-up question—I surely would have quickly realized the trick she was describing.

However, I'd gone down a completely different—and much more agonizing—road altogether. I suddenly felt like I was having an out-of-body experience. I looked down as George continued through the simple steps that always brought *The Twenty-One Card Trick* to its inevitable and satisfying conclusion. He successfully revealed Irene's chosen card and was greeted by polite applause by the rest of his tablemates.

Still feeling numb, I collected my cards and once again offered the widow my heartfelt condolences. I then stepped away from the table and scanned the room. I knew they had a buffet, but I had a more pressing question: was there also a bar of some kind?

* * *

I DIDN'T MEAN to shut the place down. It just worked out that way.

Turns out there was no bar—it was a church basement,

after all—but there was still some food left on the buffet. Although I was emotionally and physically spent from performing *The Trick That Cannot Be Explained* for over an hour, I was also hungry.

So, I grabbed the last of the sliced ham sandwiches and the remaining scoop of potato salad, speared a couple of recalcitrant pickles and a dollop of something that looked like a lime jello salad. And then I sat down, hard, at the first chair I found.

The crowd had thinned out to just a trickle of people and even these stragglers looked like they were about to head out. But I wasn't ready to go. I needed a few minutes to process what had just happened.

I was deeply mired in my thoughts when I felt a presence next to me. It was George, the fellow at Sue's table who had performed Neville's *actual* favorite card trick. He slid effortlessly into the chair next to me.

"Funerals, huh?" he finally said.

"You got that right," I agreed.

"Did you know him? Neville?"

I shook my head. "But judging by his eulogies, he was a heck of a guy."

"That he was."

We sat in silence for a few moments longer. I could see some of the catering staff starting to eye us. I think they were ready to go home and wanted us to do the same.

"That was a great card trick you did," George finally said. "Neville would have loved it."

"Yours was swell as well," I said.

George shrugged. "I saw him do that darned thing so many times, I could probably do it in my sleep. That was the thing about Neville. You hung around him enough, you just picked things up by osmosis. You didn't even realize it at the time, but you'd look back and realize he'd given you this gift. And you weren't even aware when it happened. Know what I mean?"

I looked over at George and thought about the preceding four days. About the lesson I'd had with Harry and all the practicing. And then performing that trick, that impossible trick, at table after table. And not just getting through it, but really succeeding with it.

"Yeah, I think I do," I said. "Neville was one heck of a good magician."

George and I talked about Neville for another hour, while the catering staff packed away all their gear.

We were still chatting about him long after they'd left.

THE ONE-STAR REVIEW

"'*Bumbling?*' What do they mean by 'bumbling'?"

This produced a weary sigh from Uncle Harry. "Remember when I told you never to read your reviews? This is why."

"I wasn't reading my reviews," I lied. "I was just checking my Yelp rating. I'm a businessperson. I run a business. It behooves me to have a general idea of how my work is being perceived by the public."

"In my day, we just waited to be booked again," Harry grumbled. "If you got referrals and repeat bookings, you knew your act was working. If not, you changed your act. Or got out of the business."

"Well, times have changed," I sputtered, once again scanning the on-line comments section, looking for anything else less than five stars.

"Apparently. And not for the better, it seems."

It was a rainy Saturday afternoon and for once both Harry and I were working the counter at Chicago Magic. There had been something akin to a rare 'rush' that morning—with upwards of six people in the store at the same time—but since lunch we'd had only each other for company. Which was why I had turned to my laptop and done a quick search of my name to see what the interwebs were saying about me.

It was a quick search.

My presence online is not what you would call robust. I have a Facebook page, of course, and a Twitter and Instagram account, but that's about it. You won't find me on Reddit or TikTok or SnapChat or Pinterest or whatever the new Blah-BlahBlah might be. I think I might have a LinkedIn account, but if I do, I imagine it's covered in dust and cobwebs by now.

I'm not the only Eli Marks out there, but if you add the word "magic," it does help to limit the Google results to a more reasonable number. Which is what I had done and immediately discovered the less-than positive Yelp review.

"This bumbling performer attempted to entertain us, but his magic and his patter fell far short of even your standard birthday party magician," was how it began. And it was all downhill from there. I took immediate umbrage—if that's the right word, and I'm pretty sure it was—at the unnecessary slam at birthday party magicians. Some of my best friends are birthday party magicians; I've walked a mile in their shoes, and trust me, it's no picnic.

I quickly scanned the other reviews, which—mercifully—were all five-star. But I had an overall *average* of four-point-five, which I suspected was due to that one-star review which was currently stuck in my craw.

It was short but brutal. I read it again, just to see if I'd misread the tone the first time around. I had not. After the opening salvo, it continued in the same, mean vein:

"The tricks seemed tired, as did the magician. I watched for about five minutes and then went in search of something more interesting, like maybe an old phone book to scan through. I certainly don't need to see another magician in this lifetime, that's for sure."

"Ouch."

That well-placed exhortation came from Harry, who had sidled up alongside me. He was peering down at my computer screen.

"Ouch indeed," I agreed.

"Why is it that people will see an untalented singer and not walk away from it saying, 'I'm never listening to music again'?" Harry pondered as he wandered away from the laptop. "Or see an unfunny comedian and swear off comedy? And yet, if they're subjected to one poor magic performance, that's it for magic as far as they're concerned."

"He didn't see a poor magic performance," I sputtered through gritted teeth.

"All it takes is one bad apple and they write off an entire wing of the entertainment industry."

"It was not a bad apple. It was a good apple, as evidenced by all the five-star reviews." I gestured unnecessarily at the screen, because Harry was already halfway across the small store.

"People are funny, that's for sure," he concluded as he returned to his crossword puzzle. "You just never know about them, do you?"

That last bit was rhetorical, but I wouldn't have provided an answer even if I had one.

Instead, I had clicked on the name of the one-star reviewer and started a new search. Who was this person and what would drive them to offer up such a mean-spirited assessment? In a matter of moments, I had the full name and was reading all about the unhappy critic on his Facebook page. He appeared to be a barista at a small coffee shop across town. I had never been there, but I knew where it was and how to get there.

There's no time like the present, I decided as I pulled on my windbreaker and shut my laptop. Turnabout is fair play, as Peter Marshall used to say all the time on *The Hollywood Squares*. I didn't fully understand it then and didn't really get it now, but it felt appropriate for the moment.

Turnabout is fair play indeed. It was time for this negative fellow—Billy Finch—to perhaps be on the receiving end of a one-star review of his own.

* * *

THE COFFEE SHOP was called Joe's Cuppa and it was located in a sort of no-man's land in Minneapolis: Not quite in the trendy Uptown neighborhood, not really in the industrial sector to the East, just barely on the edge of a residential section. It was hard to tell if the small building's worn façade was by design or just persistent and ongoing negligence.

I spotted Billy immediately when I came in. He was behind the counter, ringing up a coffee order while chatting with another employee. He matched his Facebook profile photo, although his wimpy goatee had filled out a bit since the picture had been taken. He still sported a man-bun, which was perched precariously atop his head. He was dressed in a faded plaid shirt with the sleeves tightly rolled up beyond the elbows of his skinny, tattoo-ladened arms.

The place wasn't huge nor was it crowded at the moment. A handful of small tables were scattered around the room and only about a quarter of them were occupied. Somewhere a speaker was pumping out some whiny indie rock classic, but by the time it reached my ears it was just white noise.

I stepped up to the counter when the previous customer moved away, waiting for Billy to spot me as the magician who ruined his otherwise strong love of magic. No such glimmer of recognition was forthcoming. He glanced up without really looking at me.

"What can I get you?"

I'm not a coffee shop sort of guy, and so I didn't have a standard order ready on the tip of my tongue. I was going to order a simple black coffee but realized if I was going to review Billy's alleged barista skills, I'd need to give him something a tad more challenging.

I had vaguely overheard the previous order, so I parroted the same phrasing the other customer had spouted, as I scanned the menu board for unique options of my own.

"Yeah, give me a cinnamon-infused free-range medium pumpkin spice latte, no foam, half soy/half almond," I said as offhandedly as I could manage.

"Sure thing," Billy said flatly. He punched numbers into the small, high tech cash register as he shouted over his shoulder. "A number four, please."

He took my name in the same disinterested manner and I swiped my credit card, bringing our short exchange to an uneventful and hasty conclusion.

I found a seat at a nearby table and popped open my laptop as I waited for Billy to mis-pronounce my name when my order was ready. Past experience had proven he had no shortage of options. 'Elly' was the most common, followed by 'Allie," although I'd heard variations as creative as 'Early,' 'Nelly,' and even 'Alfonse.'

While the order was being prepared, I made note of Billy's behavior with his co-worker and with the next customer. I realized that my plan—such as it was—had required that he have just this sort of public-facing job. There was no way I could write a review of Billy's job performance if he was a faceless drone in some bland cubicle maze in an insurance company or similar organization. I had lucked out, because his every move was on display for me to scrutinize and critique.

I was so caught up in the type of wordplay I could employ in my scathing review that I missed it the first time he called out my name. It didn't help that he pronounced it properly; I had really been on alert for a new, as-yet-unheard mispronunciation.

Rather than yell it out again to the nearly empty coffee

shop, he instead stepped around the counter and placed the cup on the table in front of me. He had even brought a couple of napkins.

"Here you go," he said. "Careful, it's hot."

Then he was gone, on his way to serve the next customer, before I could begin to sputter a response.

Recognizing I'd have to stretch the truth if I were to criticize the interaction portion of my visit, I instead turned to surveying the product Billy had put in front of me. Here was a place where I could really bring the knives out and mirror the hatchet job he had given my performance.

The only problem was, it was actually pretty tasty. The latte was just as hot as he had predicted, so I sipped carefully. I've never really gotten on the pumpkin spice bandwagon with any level of enthusiasm and I was expecting an overwhelming flood of conflicting tastes: the cinnamon fighting the pumpkin spice, while the almond and soy milk battled it out in the background.

Instead, I found a rich and smooth concoction that merely hinted at the stronger flavors, letting everything swirl together into a new taste sensation. I made a mental note to remember this order for those other rare occasions I found myself in a coffee shop.

The thought of writing notes made me turn to my laptop, where I'd opened a blank document in anticipation of my forthcoming review. So far, I'd only jotted down the name of the coffee shop and that a barista named Billy had been my server. I had anticipated listing a long string of faults and failings, with the idea of winnowing them down to a pithy assessment that would likely go quickly viral, due to its sharply cutting wit.

I stared at the nearly blank page for several moments and then took another sip of my latte. I mentally recapped the entire process from the moment I had walked into the shop, searching for any flubs or flaws I might have experienced.

Nothing was coming to mind, so I took another sip of the latte, deciding I might in fact embrace the pumpkin spice revolution if all its byproducts were as pleasing as this one.

Deciding another tactic was required, I opened the original review and clicked on Billy's avatar to scan through his other critiques, thinking I might find an 'in' to my own review by reading his past missives.

As I read his long list of assessments, I occasionally glanced up to see how he—and, by extension, his customers—were faring. There had been a steady stream of new coffee drinkers since I'd first come in. Billy and his sole co-worker were handling them all with what appeared to be a well-orchestrated process. Coffee orders were placed, pastries requested, even bags of custom-ground coffee were delivered with practiced efficiency. While his encounters with his customers were not what I would call warm, it didn't appear that anyone in the place had anything to complain about.

I turned my attention back to his previous reviews and that's where I got to see the other side of Billy Finch. It quickly became apparent my magic performance was not the outlier in his world view.

He literally didn't like anything.

A popular local restaurant was awarded a one-star review, he wrote, "because this system doesn't allow for negative numbers. If it did, I'd be using a very large negative number indeed."

A nearby co-op received its own one-star review for "employees who are as bitter as their supposedly organic produce."

A local dentist was savaged for outdated magazines in the lobby, while a theater production was criticized for not only pandering but also for its sightlines, its supposed lack of online resources, and its "unreliable air flow," whatever that meant.

Repair shops, gas stations, movie theaters, bars, pet groomers, hardware stores ... it appeared there was no category where Billy could find any product or service which met his high standards. I was surprised he didn't slam his own place of employment, but I suppose even a certified grouse such as Billy had to draw the line somewhere.

I looked up from this steady stream of negativity and watched him work for a few more minutes. While he was clearly good at his job, he didn't appear to be taking any pleasure in it. Perhaps he was one of those people who were unable to find even a glimmer of joy in the world.

I suddenly felt sad about Billy Finch and his unfortunate world view. The idea of writing a review of this depressed creature no longer held any interest for me. So, I closed the document without saving it and slid my computer into my satchel.

I downed the rest of my latte, recognizing it as the sole bright spot in this misguided adventure. As I headed out of the small coffee shop, I turned to give Billy Finch one last look. His back was to me as he poured another in a series of complicated coffee orders. His shoulders were hunched and his head was down, his posture suggesting the world was once again pressing down hard on his slim, unhappy frame.

What I didn't realize at that moment was the next time his name would appear on-line, it would not be as the byline for another of his angry one-star reviews.

It would be for his obituary.

* * *

MAGICIANS ARE OFTEN LUMPED in with other oddball performers (jugglers, clowns, fire-eaters) under the general all-purpose banner of Variety Performers. One of my favorite sub-categories from that decidedly mixed group are the ventriloquists. And, due to my uncle Harry's position in the entertainment community, I've had the pleasure of meeting my share of top-notch ventriloquists over the years.

But if I'm going to be honest, my favorite ventriloquism team are two occasional visitors to our magic shop from the Minneapolis Police Homicide division: Homicide Detective Fred Hutton and his partner, Homicide Detective Miles Wright.

Their act is simplicity itself: Homicide Detective Fred Hutton, who always nearly bangs his head on the doorway when he enters, stands silently once inside the door. His smaller and more verbal partner—trapped behind this looming Golem—then offers an unseen greeting of some sort to get the ball rolling.

For example, on this visit, it was "Morning, Marks. You got a minute?"

The effect is of a giant, grim puppet staring down at me, with a detached voice coming from somewhere behind the hulking creature.

The first couple of times it happened, I found it deeply unnerving. But now I've kind of come to look forward to it. I'm not saying they'd make it past the audition round on *America's Got Talent*, but it amuses me to no end.

"Ah, yes," I said, not even attempting to soften my grin. "The comedy stylings of Hutton & Wright."

It's a joke I've used before, but what makes it truly interesting is that it's the only time I ever referred to the large man by anything but his full name and title. Although he's actually a pretty sharp detective, I'm not sure he's ever noticed this small detail.

Here's the thing: Many divorced men don't have to deal—on a frequent basis—with their ex-wife's new husband. Sadly, I am one of the few who does. Our relationship has always been, at best, frosty; we've kept things cordial, but I sincerely doubt it will ever rise to anything you might call warm.

Because of this coolness between us—and probably also due to Homicide Detective Fred Hutton's natural taciturn disposition—his partner generally did most of the talking in our encounters. Which Miles Wright attempted to do, just as soon as he was able to push his way into the store.

"How's business?" Wright said sarcastically as he glanced around the empty magic shop. "Having a fire sale?"

"No, but sadly we're out of joy buzzers and fake vomit," I said. "So, I'm afraid you'll have to look elsewhere for your supplies."

"You're a funny man."

"There is debate on that," I said quietly. "What can I do for you?"

"We're investigating a recent murder," Wright said as he plopped a bulky police-issue laptop computer on the counter between us. "A fellow got himself shot coming home from work earlier this week."

"A mugging?" I suggested.

Wright shook his head. "If it was, it wasn't a particularly successful one. Victim's wallet was untouched, as was his fancy phone and a few contraband substances we found on his person."

He opened the computer and skillfully used the track pad to open a folder and then scanned through some files.

"It happened by the backdoor to his apartment building, about an hour after he'd left work. No CCTV at the apartment, but we did get the video files from his place of employment. So we scanned through the events of the day he got shot. And who do we find seated at one of the tables? And not just sitting there, but clearly watching the victim's every move."

He spun the laptop around and gestured toward the image on the screen, but I already had a pretty good idea what I'd see.

It was a high angle, black and white shot of the room. There I was, seated at a table at Joe's Cuppa, practically staring at the barista as he worked.

"How do you know Billy Finch?" These were the first words out of Homicide Detective Fred Hutton's mouth since they'd walked in. "And why did you spend nearly an hour watching him the day he was shot?"

"Well, obviously I didn't know he was going to be shot while I was there," I began, but Wright cut me off.

"That's not obvious at all. So why were you there and what was your interest in the victim?"

I supposed I could have hemmed and hawed, but I've found that the truth—while occasionally painful—is generally the shortest distance between two points. Plus, I wasn't keen on the idea of being a murder suspect one second longer than necessary.

So, I moved down the counter to where my laptop was positioned and did some quick swiping and clicking of my own. The two men followed me. By the time they arrived I had found the review. I spun the laptop around so they could see the screen.

"I got a one-star review—a rare one-star review, I might add —and I decided to check the guy out. Maybe write a mean-spirited review of my own."

"Isn't that a bit, I don't know," Wright said, clearly struggling to find the right word. "Petty?"

"It's probably the definition of petty," I agreed. "Look, I'm not proud of it, but that's the truth. I went into the shop to see if he was bad at his job so I could write about it on-line."

"The way he wrote about how you're bad at your job?" Homicide Detective Fred Hutton's face registered the slightest smile as he said this.

"I'm not bad at my job," I snapped. My attempt to take any defensiveness out of my tone had failed miserably. "And, as it turns out, he's not so bad at his job either. Or, at least, he was."

In an effort to take the focus off my petty nature, I moved back down the counter to their laptop, which was still running the video from the coffee shop.

"So, do you have any leads?"

Homicide Detective Fred Hutton continued to scan through the review on my computer. Wright shook his head as he followed me. "Nothing to write home about. But he clearly ticked somebody off."

"Or was in the wrong place at the wrong time," I suggested.

Wright shrugged. "Maybe, but it doesn't feel like that. I think he was the target."

"What's that on the bottom of the screen?" I gestured toward text which was scrolling in one corner of the monitor.

"Whatever fast-talker sold this coffee shop their CCTV system had a nice payday on this one," Wright said with a grim chuckle. "It's much more sophisticated than they needed, that's for sure."

Recognizing Wright hadn't really answered my question, Homicide Detective Fred Hutton turned from his position at the other end of the counter.

"It's connected to the cash register," he said flatly. "It monitors purchases."

"It's so the store can make sure that what's being rung up is actually what's being sold," Wright added. "It's really designed for larger retail environments. You know: your Targets, your Walmarts. The Loss Prevention guys monitor all the cash registers and look for anomalies."

My expression must have adequately reflected my confusion, so Wright continued.

"Like, I heard of this one case where a cashier taped the UPC code from a pack of gum to the palm of his hand," he continued. "A buddy comes up with a TV or some other big-ticket item and the cashier appears to scan it—everyone hears the beep and all that—but he actually ends up charging the guy for just a pack of gum. And his pal walks out with a TV."

"But the Loss Prevention Guys can see on the video that the customer is being charged for a pack of gum and getting a TV instead," I said.

"If they happen to be looking at that moment, sure," Wright said. "But odds are good they might miss it."

"Sounds pretty foolproof."

"It is, unless you're a fool," Homicide Detective Fred Hutton said. He appeared to have finished reading Billy Finch's review and was headed down the counter toward us. "A fellow may get away with that once, maybe twice, but the smart crook learns to space these things out."

"Yeah, but instead most of those idiots just go whole hog. Like, they'll let a buddy buy a cart full of electronics for the price of twenty packs of gum," Wright said, grinning at the image. "That sends up a lot of red flags and before they know it, they're out of a job, convicted of grand larceny and rolling on the grey goose, doing two-and-a-half to five."

I nodded as I looked down at the video image of the transactions taking place at Joe's Cuppa. "You're right, this system seems like overkill," I agreed.

"There's one born every minute," Wright said.

I looked up at the two men. Their suits, though obviously different sizes, appeared to be nearly identical in every other way. I was tempted to question them further on this point, but I had a more pressing question.

"You guys don't actually think I had anything to do with this, do you?"

They stared back at me, a study in blank faces. And then after what seemed like a long time, Wright smiled and shook his head.

"No, not really," he said. "However, you did pop up on the

video and Fred here says the joint next door has good burgers. So we thought we'd kill two birds, as it were. Is it true?"

He'd lost me. "Is what true?"

"The joint next door," he said with a cock of his head. "Are their burgers worth the drive from downtown?"

I shrugged. "Well, they claim to have the world's best Juicy Lucy, but so do three other bars in town. However, they make decent fries and if you use a little caution, their Juicy Lucy can do the trick."

"Caution?"

"The cheese inside the Juicy Lucy is usually about 400 degrees Fahrenheit by the time it reaches the table, so take care with that first bite," I explained. I was glad the topic had shifted away from my potential involvement in a recent homicide to the more benign topic of the alleged superiority of the burger next door.

"Thanks." Wright reached for the laptop, but I put my hand on it first.

"Do you mind if I look at the video for a bit? While you have lunch?" I wasn't sure why, but there was obviously nothing else going on in the store and so any distraction, regardless of how mundane, had a certain appeal.

"Sure thing," Wright said with a shrug. "We'll grab it on our way back."

Homicide Detective Fred Hutton appeared less enamored with the concept. But he said nothing as the two men left the shop, heading toward a greasy yet satisfying lunch next door.

* * *

IF I WAS LOOKING for a monotonous endeavor, I had found it.

Sitting in the coffee shop in real time hadn't been a thrill a minute, but re-watching the action from this high, slightly fuzzy angle was near sleep inducing.

The initial fascination of observing a transaction taking place and simultaneously seeing the purchase information appearing as text in the lower corner of the screen quickly waned. It may have been because the store offered a limited supply of products and a predictable repetition quickly set in.

Yet I had to admit there was an odd, appealing rhythm to the process: The semi-steady flow of customers, the quick exchanges, the coffee served, the bags of coffee delivered, the pastries distributed.

Maybe it was because I was sitting in an empty magic store just a few miles away, with no customers, no steady stream of transactions, no persistent tabulating of cash register receipts. Maybe I was just living vicariously, seeing what it might be like to oversee a thriving, probably profitable enterprise.

Was that why I kept watching?

I glanced around our small, dusty shop. It always felt like there was a light out, somewhere in the room, but it wasn't readily apparent just where. The displays in the front window blocked what little sun that side of the building got, while the fluorescents over the counters offered the bare minimum of light they could without actually being off.

I turned my attention back to the video of the bright, busy coffee shop, focusing my attention on Billy Finch's swift and efficient moves. There was no wasted motion, as he glided from the register to the coffee machines to the small bakery display to the rack holding bags of coffee. He was, I had to admit, quite good at his job.

And that high tech cash register certainly helped to keep things moving. People inserted—or merely—touched their credit cards to a box on the counter or used their phones, and the sales popped up instantly on the screen.

I glanced over at our own cash register, which would probably be considered an antique in most quarters, with its hard-to-press keys and a cash drawer desperately in need of oiling. I had been in the shop the day an equipment salesman had tried to interest Uncle Harry with a newer model, similar to what they were using at Joe's Cuppa. He'd extolled the machine's ease of use, explaining that it allowed for three or four times as many sales an hour. Harry nearly laughed the poor man out of the store.

"I find it hard to believe," Harry said as he showed him the door, "that a mere cash register is going to increase our foot traffic in any appreciable way. And if it did, then I'd get out of magic and into the cash register business. Good day, sir."

The door was then closed as firmly as Harry's mind on the topic.

I turned my attention back to the video playing on Wright's laptop. And I started to play a little game: Guess the Purchase.

Could I guess what a customer would buy, based only on the way they approached the counter? I certainly couldn't hear them and my view of them was limited to what they looked like from behind.

That guy's going to get a mocha latte, I would think.

Wrong. Black coffee and a croissant.

That woman looks like the iced coffee type.

Bingo. Iced coffee it was.

This fellow is just there to buy a bag of ground coffee.

Right again!

While I'm estimating my overall correct guesses fell far below fifty percent, I celebrated the successes and let the failures recede quickly into the murky past. It's a technique that makes popular psychics successful, and it worked just as well for me in this situation.

And then I noticed it.

But what did I notice? I scanned the video back and re-watched the purchase, which was typical in all ways but one. I watched the next purchase and the five after that, then scanned back to several earlier purchases. And then scanned ahead to the one that had caught my eye.

A song from my childhood played in the distant recesses of my brain.

One of these things is not like the other. One of these things just doesn't belong.

* * *

"MARKS, you were right about that first bite of the Juicy Lucy. Sadly, I'd forgotten your warning until the very moment that molten cheese hit the tip of my tongue. Never again!"

Miles Wright was nearly shouting this at me as he strolled back into our shop. Homicide Detective Fred Hutton followed him in moments later; as usual, he was as quiet as his partner was loud.

I'm guessing the look of intensity on my face as I studied the computer screen was lost on Wright, but his partner picked up on it instantly.

"What have you found?" Homicide Detective Fred Hutton said. His tone was a peculiar mix of both optimism and accusation.

"Let me ask this: Did Billy Finch have more money in his bank account than you might have expected?"

Miles Wright was suddenly all business. "He sure did," he said. "And more cash in his apartment than your typical barista should have stashed away."

"I'm not surprised." I turned my attention back to the video, where I was re-watching the moment where the two employees closed up the shop and locked the front door. Although the video would continue to monitor the empty shop throughout the night, a quick scan had shown the place remained unoccupied until one of the employees opened it up early the next morning.

Of course, that employee hadn't been Billy Finch. At that point, he'd been dead for about eight hours.

"It's this purchase here, at 2:37 p.m.," I said as I spun the laptop to give the two cops a better view. "You can see from the readout on the screen, it's for a twelve-ounce bag of whole bean Dark French Roast coffee. If I'm reading the abbreviations correctly."

They studied the screen as—from our high-angle vantage point—Billy Finch rang up the order. The purchase information appeared on the lower right corner of the screen as Billy turned and headed into the back room. A few moments later, he returned with the small pre-packaged bag of coffee, handing it to the customer along with the printed receipt.

The whole thing had taken less than a minute. And then Billy Finch was onto the next customer.

Wright ran a hand through his thinning hair. "I don't get it," he said. "What are we looking at?"

I spun the computer around and began to scan to another moment from the video file.

"My uncle Harry has a trick he does in his act, in his cabaret show. I won't go into the details of how it works, but in order for the trick to be successful, he has to put his hands on his hips. Just for a second. But if he doesn't do that, the trick won't work."

I looked up from my scanning. The two men stared back at me.

"So, in order to make sure this particular move doesn't stand out, Harry does this really smart thing." I glanced at the screen and then back at the cops, on the off chance they might have guessed what that smart thing was. Their expressions suggested they weren't getting ahead of me.

"What Harry does," I continued, "is that up until that point in the act—and several times later in the show—he puts his hands on his hips. He doesn't make any reference to it, he just does it. Consequently, the audience gets used to it; they understand it's just a habit of his."

"So, when he <u>has to</u> put his hands on his hips, they don't notice anything out of the ordinary," Wright said brightly.

"Bingo," I agreed. "However, our friend Billy Finch clearly doesn't know that trick. Here he is selling that exact same product—a twelve-ounce bag of Dark French Roast whole beans—to a customer ten minutes earlier."

They studied the screen as Billy rang up the order, stepped over to a shelf loaded with small bags of coffee, grabbed one and handed it to the customer along with the receipt.

I scanned the video quickly forward.

"And here he is again, fifteen minutes later, selling that same product to another customer."

Once again, Billy rang up the order, grabbed a bag of coffee from the shelf behind him, and handed it to the customer along with the receipt.

"He does the same thing six more times before the shop closes," I said as I hit the 'pause' button. "And five times earlier in the day. Each time, he always takes the product from the shelf behind him."

"However, at 2:37, he went into the back room to get the same product," Homicide Detective Fred Hutton said quietly.

"So, I'm betting it wasn't actually the same product," Wright added.

I nodded. "I think so. It was likely some sort of exchange for a product that, odds are, *wasn't* coffee."

"Indeed," Homicide Detective Fred Hutton agreed.

"And the best part is," I continued as I pointed at the screen, "the customer used a credit card. It's noted here, right under the product information on the screen. And if that cash register is anything like the one some guy tried to sell Uncle Harry, you'll have a complete record of the purchase, including any name and address associated with the credit card he used."

"Assuming it wasn't a stolen credit card," Wright grumbled.

"True enough," I said. I closed the computer and pushed it toward him. "But you now have more than what you had when you walked in here an hour ago. Plus a burned tongue and a lesson well learned."

Their silence as they exited the shop suggested that, on at least one level, they agreed with me.

* * *

"WELL, Marks. When you're right, you're right."

Harry looked up from his position behind the counter as Homicide Detective Miles Wright shut the shop door behind him.

"I've been saying that about myself for years," Harry said. "It's nice that the rest of you are finally starting to catch on."

"I think he's actually talking about me," I said as I came through the curtain which separated the back room from the rest of the magic store. I'd been working on my laptop and I set it on the counter in front of me.

"Indeed, I am," Wright said. He was grinning ear to ear. "I was just in the neighborhood to grab my new favorite Juicy Lucy and I thought I'd give you the good news in person: We found the guy who shot Billy Finch."

"Fantastic," I said. "And was it related to that odd-ball coffee purchase?"

"It was indeedly-doo," he said. I couldn't tell if his excitement was because of the news he was delivering or his impending Juicy Lucy. "Turns out, our friend Mr. Finch was moving product for a local drug dealer and he decided to branch out and start his own enterprise. To fund it, he was skimming a little off the top. Literally. He was taking small portions of the product—heroin, as it turns out—with the idea of selling it with another guy."

Wright leaned on the counter as he continued his explanation. "What we witnessed on the video was a hand-off of the
product to that associate who was going to re-sell what they'd
skimmed. Then they'd split the proceeds. Turns out, though,
that word got back to the top guy and he decided to send a
message to his crew: No freelancing allowed."

"Well, Billy certainly got that message. Was it the credit card
information that did the trick?"

"It was, it was. The exchange at the coffee shop was to
throw off any compatriots who might be watching. You know, a
guy comes in, buys a bag of coffee, walks out. Who's going to
think anything of that? The problem was, the fool Billy was
working with used his own credit card. When we told him he
was implicated in a first-degree murder case, he accepted a plea
deal and spilled all the beans. And I'm not just talking coffee
beans."

"What I don't get is this," I said as I pulled up a stool. "Why
leave a trail like that with a credit card? Why not just use cash
for the exchange? It was all of what, twelve bucks?"

"I asked him that very question and you will appreciate the
irony of his answer," Wright said. "He said he and Billy
discussed it and decided it would be more suspicious to use
cash, because nobody uses cash anymore. They felt it would
make their little exchange stand out more. Hence, the credit
card."

He turned to Uncle Harry. "It's like that 'hands on hip thing'
you do in your act," Wright said.

To reinforce the concept, he dramatically placed his hands
on his hips.

Harry stared back at him blankly. "Excuse me?"

I stepped in to assist Wright by putting my hands on my
own hips. "You know," I said. "That hip thing you do. In your
act."

Harry turned to me and then back to Wright. "What are

you, drunk? You both look like you're about to break into a rendition of *I'm a Little Teapot*, for goodness sake!"

I dropped my hands and stepped over to where Harry was seated. I leaned in and whispered a few words in his ear. Once he'd heard enough, he pushed me away.

"Goodness, I haven't performed that trick in that way in at least twenty years," he growled. "And, while we're on the subject, why are you spilling my trade secrets to the laity?"

"Concepts, not specifics," I said. "Educational use only."

"Well, I should hope so," Harry said as he returned his attention to his crossword puzzle.

"Anyway, thanks for the help on this one," Wright said as he headed back toward the door. "And for the tip on that Juicy Lucy. I can practically taste it right now."

"Careful of that first bite," Harry and I said in unison.

Wright nodded. "Thanks, but I carry a constant reminder on the tip of my tongue." He made a vague gesture toward his mouth, the motion morphing into a wave as he stepped through the door.

"Helping out our friends in blue again?" Harry said, peering at me over his glasses.

"Not doing anything you wouldn't do," I countered.

"Indeed, indeed," he muttered. "And the victim he mentioned? That was the fellow who gave you the shabby review?"

"He was indeed."

"Well, I don't want to speak ill of the dead, but based on the little I heard of his nefarious plan, I would be hard pressed to give it anything higher than one star."

"Speaking of poor notices," I said as I flipped open my laptop. "I was doing a quick search and came across yet another one-star review."

"Eli, what have I told you about reading your bad reviews," Harry began, but I cut him off.

"No, this wasn't for magician Eli Marks. I found a nasty review for a magician named *Harry* Marks."

His eyebrows shot up. "What? A one-star review? For me? Nonsense."

"Pretty recent, too," I added as I scanned the online critique.

"Let me see that," Harry said as he began to climb down from his stool.

"But what about not reading reviews?"

"That was a suggestion, not an edict. Now let me see that review."

"Not on your life," I said with a laugh.

I may not be fleet of foot, but I'm fleeter than an eighty-year-old man, that's for sure. I had my laptop closed and under my arm in a jiffy.

In fact, I wager I was up a full flight of stairs toward my apartment before Harry was even halfway across the store.

THE VANISHING MAN (REDUX)

"In my experience, law enforcement folks aren't usually a good audience for magic."

"Why do you think that is?" I was multitasking behind the bar, topping off Uncle Harry's ginger ale while also filling a new pitcher of beer.

"Because they can never really enjoy the trick until they figure out how it was done."

I shrugged as I handed Harry his ginger ale. "I guess. But you could say the same for many magicians."

"True enough," Harry agreed.

He turned and looked across the room at the two disparate groups who made up the sum total of my customers on this dark and cloudy afternoon.

Harry's table consisted of two of the gang of aging magicians collectively known as The Minneapolis Mystics. They'd been meeting here weekly in various combinations over the years, trading lies and embellishing exaggerations since I was a kid. I had literally learned magic at their feet. Today's assembly, which hardly qualified as a quorum, consisted only of Harry and his friend, mentalist Abe Ackerman.

Two tables and a million miles away sat a handful of law enforcement folks who Harry had dubbed The Four Horseman of Criminal Apprehension. I'm not sure why they had picked my bar as their meeting spot, beyond the fact that one of them —Homicide Detective Fred Hutton—was now married to my ex-wife. It wasn't because he and I were pals; history had demonstrated just the opposite. At best, you could say he tolerated my existence, and the feeling was mutual.

And yet he and his cronies had chosen this spot for their weekly get-togethers. And who was I to discourage them? They spoke quietly, drank moderately and tipped to excess, so in my mind they were welcome additions.

I grabbed the full pitcher and a fresh bowl of filberts and headed over to their table, arriving just as one of them, Glenn Randolph, was wrapping up his story.

"So, apparently this idiot had cut just one corner each off four twenty-dollar bills. He then glued each of the pieces to the front of a one-dollar bill, and to be honest it didn't look bad. He hands it to the clerk to pay for his pack of gum, and she gives him back change for a one. Our guy looks at it and says, 'Hey, I'm short here. I gave you a twenty!' And she points to the bill in her hand and says, 'It's a one.' And this genius says, 'No, no, you have to turn it over.'"

The table responded with knowing laughter, each of them probably thinking back to one or more incompetent criminals they'd nabbed over the years.

"Of course, nowadays, with credit cards and smart phones, that sort of scam has gone the way of the Pony Express," Randolph continued, finishing the remains of his beer as he reached for the new pitcher.

Like my ex-wife's new husband, Randolph was a Detective with the Minneapolis Police Department, working primarily in the Robbery and Financial Crimes Division. If he resembled an aging wrestler, it was probably because he was. He had ranked nationally while in college. Gravity and aging may have had their way with him, but he still occasionally displayed the grace of an athlete in his movements.

He finished filling his glass and looked up at me. "I suppose smart phones have done a number on magic as well," he said with a grin. "I mean, when you've got a miracle machine in your hand, who needs card tricks, am I right?"

He turned to the others and received knowing laughs in return, with the exception of Homicide Detective Fred Hutton, who only offered up a dim smile.

"Magicians have proven to be pretty adept at quickly adapting to new technology," I said as I pulled my phone from my pocket. "But you're right: who needs a deck of cards when you have a smart phone." I held mine up, revealing the image on the screen was of a deck of blue-backed playing cards. I looked over at Randolph. "Think of a card."

He glanced around the table, not sure how he should be reacting to this impromptu performance. He stuttered, but before he could answer, he was beaten to the punch.

"Three of diamonds." This came from Carol Hollinger, who ran the Minneapolis Police Department's forensics lab. She was probably the smartest one of the quartet and certainly the nicest. Although she dressed like a middle-aged librarian, she had a quick wit and an impressive lexicon of profanity when the situation warranted it.

"Three of diamonds? Funny, I was thinking of that very same card," I said as I held the phone out for them. I passed my hand briefly over the device. They looked down to see the image on the screen was now the three of diamonds, face up on the deck.

This produced a delighted giggle from Carol and a grunt of disbelief from Randolph.

"It's voice-activated," he said with a sneer. "Siri heard Carol or you say the name of the card."

"Or maybe it's using the gyroscopic technology in the phone," offered Mark Kelly, the fourth member of the group. He wasn't strictly in law enforcement but considered himself law enforcement-adjacent. He was a former cop who was now an investigator for a top insurance company. "You know, you tilt the phone this way or that, to make a certain card appear."

"I don't know, why don't you check out the card for yourself," I suggested. In a quick motion, I pulled a real card off the phone and handed it to him, flipping it over so they all could see both sides before he took it for a closer examination.

"In fact, if you want," I continued, "feel free to examine the entire deck."

With that, I pushed my thumb against the object in my hands, revealing that it was now a complete deck of cards. I did a quick spread of the cards—showing that not only were they real cards, but also all different—before letting them fall in a cascade to the tabletop.

This produced a yelp of laughter from Carol Hollinger, while a mystified Mark Kelly continued to examine the three of diamonds I'd handed him. He held it like it was some sort of alien object, slowly turning it over, scrutinizing both sides.

Seeing they already had two full bowls of filberts, I picked up their empty pitcher and stopped at Harry's table to leave the extra bowl on my way back to the bar.

"I would imagine," Harry said as he turned to the neighboring group, "that new technology has forced even your stupidest criminals to get a little bit smarter. You know, with DNA and cell phone towers and triangulating locations and latent fingerprints and forensic carbon-14 dating, criminals must have to work a lot harder nowadays."

"Harry, are you just listing words you've heard on *CSI Miami*?" Carol Hollinger said with a laugh.

"Perhaps," Harry admitted. "But as your technology improves, don't your criminals have to get smarter as well?"

"You'll be relieved to know that today's criminals are just as stupid as they've always been," she continued as she glanced around her table for confirmation. "And, from my experience, the smarter they think they are, the easier they are to catch."

"The same is true in the magic world," offered Abe Ackerman as he daintily picked out the largest filberts in the new bowl. "The smartest audience members are usually the easiest to fool, because they always think they're two steps ahead of you."

"When they're often four steps behind," Harry agreed.

"That's not to say we still don't run into an occasional situation which simply baffles us," Carol said. "Like the Drescher Diamond case."

Randolph and Kelly nodded and grunted in agreement, shaking their heads at the memory.

"Sounds intriguing," Harry said as he leaned forward in his chair. "The Drescher Diamond case you say? Details, please."

The small group exchanged looks, not immediately warming to this idea.

"It was in all the papers," Carol finally said with a shrug.

"I suppose it was," Glenn Randolph agreed. He turned to Harry and Abe. "Cal Drescher's hotel room was broken into and his wife's diamond necklace—"

"Valued at $250,000," Carol added.

"Yes," Randolph continued. "Her valuable necklace was stolen."

Harry looked at him expectantly. "Surely there was more to it than that?"

"The necklace vanished from their hotel room. There was no way in, no way out. But while the couple was at dinner, someone—somehow—got in and took it."

"Assuming it was stolen at all," Mark Kelly added quickly.

"The insurance company questioned the validity of the claim?" Harry asked.

"In the strongest possible terms," Kelly said. "There was no proof the necklace was stolen."

"The room was ransacked," Carol offered.

"The couple could have easily done that before they left," Kelly shot back. "Personally, I wouldn't put it past them. A shady pair, both of them."

"Upstanding citizens," Carol countered.

"Yes, the worst kind," Kelly said as he reached for a refill.

"Here's what went down," Randolph said, settling back in his chair as he began to recount the story. "Cal and Denise Drescher were staying overnight at a ritzy hotel in downtown Minneapolis. You know, that high-end one down by Loring Park? They were in town for the night to attend a charity event in the hotel's ballroom.

"They checked in about three o'clock and, according to everyone at the front desk, they were bickering from the moment they arrived. She was ticked off about his driving, he was mad she had brought three suitcases for a one-night stay. They went on and on.

"There were two clerks on duty at the time, a long-time employee named Josh White, and a new trainee named Nicole Swanson. The manager, Steve Harrington and the concierge, Maria Lopez, were also within earshot and heard the entire conversation."

"Their individual testimony is remarkably consistent," Kelly agreed.

"It must have been pretty memorable for all four to distinctly remember it," Harry commented.

"Well, when she took out the honking big diamond necklace, they really sat up and took notice," Randolph said. "Denise pulled this huge hunk of jewelry out of her purse, saying she thought they should put it in the hotel safe for the night. Cal Drescher countered he thought she had brought it along to wear it; if not, why bring it? She said she still hadn't decided what she was wearing. Back and forth they went. She ends up putting it back into her purse and off they go to the elevators."

"So, at that point, the witnesses have established the necklace was on her person," Mark Kelly added. He was still twirling the three of diamonds between his fingers.

"Not only the witnesses but the CCTV footage from the lobby as well," Randolph continued. "CCTV also shows them getting off the elevator on the sixteenth floor and heading down the hall to their room. Two hours later, we've got footage of them exiting their room, dressed for the fancy charity event downstairs. Dressed to the nines. Except she's not wearing the necklace."

"So, she decided against wearing it?" Abe Ackerman asked. He appeared to have succeeded in picking the largest filberts from the bowl.

"According to the Dreschers, there was an argument about her wardrobe," Randolph explained. "In his statement, Cal Drescher said he gave the incorrect response when his wife asked if her first choice of outfit made her look fat."

"There's only one right answer to that question," Harry said with a chuckle.

"Yeah, well Cal picked the wrong one, which resulted in Denise abandoning that outfit for another one. And this one, she said, wasn't a good match for the diamond necklace. So, she left it in the room, hiding it inside a toiletry bag buried in one of her three suitcases."

"But certainly there was an in-room safe of some kind?" Harry said.

"Indeed there was," Randolph agreed. "However, according to the couple, there had been an 'incident' in the past when Cal Drescher employed an in-room safe and then forgot the combination he'd made up. From that point on, Denise had put a ban on their use."

"Once bitten, as it were," Abe mumbled to no one in particular. "So, they head down to the party and the video footage in the hallway shows her not wearing the diamond necklace?"

Abe gave me a wave and pointed to his drink and the half-full filbert bowl. I had been sitting on a stool at the bar, but jumped down to handle his request while Randolph continued the story.

"Exactly," he said. "And the video footage also shows that no one went in or out of that room until the Dreschers got back about four hours later."

"And I should point out, we've checked the meta data on the footage and there was no monkey business," Carol Hollinger added. "The movements of guests and staff up and down that hall corresponded perfectly with footage from the elevators and stairwells. In short, no one tampered with the CCTV footage."

"And no one went into their room," Randolph continued. "That's documented by the footage and confirmed by the electronic lock on the door. According to the log, the lock was unlocked with their key card when they arrived at 3:23 p.m. and then unlocked again, with the same card, at 11:41 p.m."

"When did they report the diamond necklace had gone missing?" I asked. I had returned with Abe's drink and a fresh bowl of filberts.

"Five minutes later," Randolph said. "They took one look at their ransacked room, determined the necklace was gone and called 911."

"And there's no adjoining room or balcony?" I asked as I pulled up a chair at Harry's table.

Randolph shook his head. "No adjoining room, no connecting doors, no balcony. They were sixteen stories up and the windows don't open. The only way in was through that one door."

"And yet someone got in, ransacked the room and took the diamond necklace," I said.

"Or they staged it," Mark Kelly offered. "Classic insurance scam. I've seen it a million times."

Randolph shook his head slowly. "Maybe," he said. "I've interviewed my share of liars, and I wasn't getting that vibe from this couple. And, I don't know. The room really *felt* like someone had gone through it, searching for something."

"Intuition?" Harry offered.

Randolph shrugged. "After a while, you get a sense for these things."

Harry turned to Carol Hollinger. "And forensics agreed?"

"For the most part," she said. "Whoever it was, they did a real number on the room. All the drawers had been gone through. Even the medicine cabinet was in a shambles, although there was nothing in it large enough to hold the necklace. And, for some reason, they'd squeezed all the toothpaste out of the tube."

"Excuse me?" Harry said as he leaned forward.

"Yes, the contents of a tube of toothpaste had been squirted on the sink and the adjacent counter. I can't imagine they were looking for the necklace inside of it, though."

Harry considered this for a long moment and then turned to Mark Kelly. "And, from an insurance perspective, you think the whole thing was staged?"

"What am I supposed to think," Kelly said. "The proof is in the CCTV footage and the log for the electronic lock: No one went in or out of that room while the Dreschers were gone. A clear case of fraud, if you ask me."

Harry looked over at Abe. "Doesn't this remind you of *The Vanishing Man*?"

Abe nodded. "That's the first thing I thought of," he said. "Virtually the same set-up."

"What's *The Vanishing Man*?" This came from Homicide

Detective Fred Hutton, who had silently been listening all this time.

"It's a story from way back," Harry said. "In 1950, the Society of American Magicians and the International Brotherhood of Magicians held a joint conference at a big hotel. I think it was in Boston."

Abe shook his head. "Cleveland, I'm sure of it," he said. "Or maybe Philadelphia."

"Wherever it was," Harry continued, "one of the attendees performed a trick for a bunch of other magicians in his hotel room. It's an illusion which has come to be known as *The Vanishing Man*."

"What's the trick?" Randolph said.

"Simplicity itself," Harry said. "The audience assembled in the hallway outside his hotel room. And, I should add, the room was similarly configured to the one in your case: Only one way in, no adjoining doors, no open windows. A classic locked room."

"Classic," Abe agreed.

"Our magician went into the room, with instructions to the assembled that they had 30 minutes to find where he was hiding. And at the end of that 30 minutes, they would vacate the room and he would re-appear."

"And did he?" Randolph asked.

"He did, just as promised," Harry said with a grin. "They searched the room for thirty minutes and he was nowhere to be found. No secret panels under the vanity, no trapdoors in the closet, no tunnels discovered under the bed. At the end of thirty minutes, they left the room. And five minutes later, the door opened. And out he stepped."

"If that's not a miracle, I don't know what is," Abe said. "Of course, not to be outdone, Harry did his own variation on the effect years later."

"A minor effort," he said modestly. "It was really my pal David Williamson's idea. I just put my own spin on it."

I was genuinely intrigued. "I've never heard about this," I said. I thought I had heard every one of my uncle Harry's stories, many of them multiple times. But this was a new one to me.

"Oh, it was silly, really," Harry said with a chuckle. "It was back at Magic Live, a long time ago. I announced to a group that I was going to recreate *The Vanishing Man* effect at such-and-such a time. Very portentous, you know."

"So, we all show up in the hall outside his hotel room at the appointed hour," Abe added. "There were a bunch of us."

"I addressed the group and said I was going to attempt it, but that I felt I could probably only pull off the effect for twenty minutes or so," Harry explained. "I said they could come in, one at a time, and they would each have four minutes to search the room in their attempt to find me. Then I went into the room."

"We waited five minutes and then we started the clock," Abe said, picking up the story. "The first magician goes in. Four minutes later he comes out, shaking his head. 'He's gone,' the guy says. 'Disappeared.'

"Then the next one and the next one," Abe continued. "Same reaction every time. Complete mystification. By this point, my curiosity is piqued. Finally, it's my turn. I go into the room. The curtains are drawn and there is a lamp on by the bed. There is light coming from the bathroom. But the room appears empty."

Abe's voice had gotten quieter as he recounted his tale, so the folks at the adjacent table leaned in to hear him.

"He's not behind the curtains, he's not in the closet, he's not in—or under—the bed," Abe said, ticking off the locations on his fingers as he listed them. "It's not a big room. Which left only the bathroom. So, I push the door open and the first thing

I see is my reflection in the mirror. And then I pull back the shower curtain and what do you think I see?"

"Nothing?" Carol Hollinger said breathlessly.

"No, I see Harry," Abe said with an abrupt laugh. "He's standing there in the tub, big as life. He grins at me, puts a finger to his lips and says ..."

"'Tell them you couldn't find me,'" Harry said in a hoarse whisper.

Abe laughed at the memory. "So, just like everyone else who'd come through the room, I go back out into the hallway and announce that I can't find him. And as the next guy goes in to try his luck, I exchanged a look with the first magician. We give each other the slightest of winks. We're in the club."

"They all did a great job," Harry said between laughs. He was close to crying from the memory.

"But the beauty part," Abe said, catching his breath. "The beauty part was that at the end of twenty minutes, Harry came out of the room. He told the group he was exhausted; he couldn't do it anymore. But there were still four or five guys who never got to go into the room. Not only were they disappointed, but they'd just heard seven or eight guys tell them that Harry Marks had vanished in that hotel room. And they bought it. They believed that he had pulled off *The Vanishing Man.*"

"When did you set them straight?" I asked. I couldn't believe I had never heard this story from Harry before.

"A year from never," Abe said as he uttered another barking laugh.

"What?"

Harry shook his head, still laughing. "No, we never told them. The ones who went into the room kept the faith. It was a thing of beauty. I give credit to David Williamson for the idea, of course. But we pulled it off gorgeously."

"Talk about the long con," Glenn Randolph said, a distinct tone of admiration in his voice.

"Indeed," I agreed. "*The Vanishing Man, Redux.*"

"Magicians are still talking about it," Abe said as he held up his glass and toasted Harry.

"That's all well and good," Mark Kelly said quickly. "But you haven't explained how the first guy did the trick and how it connects with the Drescher case?"

"Ah, yes," Harry said catching his breath. "I'm afraid we have gone off on a bit of a tangent."

"That's what we do," Abe mumbled as he took a long sip. "Otherwise, what's the point?"

"This is just a theory, of course," Harry continued. "But I believe the method used to <u>get out</u> of the hotel room in *The Vanishing Man* may have been similar to the one employed to <u>get into</u> the room in your case. Here's how our fellow did it back in the day.

"He had discovered, entirely by chance, that the medicine cabinet in his room had not been attached, but merely set into a recess in the wall. He pulled it out, revealing a crawl space of some kind. Probably a maintenance shaft for ventilation. But certainly large enough to hide in, if only for 30 minutes or so. Which is what he proceeded to do. He set up the situation with the group in the hallway, entered the room and disappeared behind the medicine cabinet, pulling it back into position from inside the ventilation shaft. And thus, *The Vanishing Man* effect was born."

"Wait," Mark Kelly said as he held up a hand. "Are you saying the thief or thieves were hiding in the wall of the hotel room?"

Harry shook his head. "By no means," he said quickly. "And this is, of course, just a theory. First let me ask you this: Does anyone know if the Dreschers received their room key before or after Denise Drescher pulled the diamond necklace out of her purse?"

"As I recall," Glenn Randolph offered, "Denise Drescher

took the necklace out of her purse early in the check-in process."

"Excellent," Harry said. "I think seeing that valuable piece of jewelry triggered a plan that may have been in the offing for quite some time. Our thief was just waiting for the right target. When they spotted the necklace, they decided they had found what they'd been waiting for. The first step was to ensure the Dreschers were placed in one specific room in the hotel which had been fitted out for this eventuality."

"That narrows the suspects down to the two desk clerks," Randolph said. "Josh White or Nicole Swanson."

"The thief would likely have worked at the hotel for a while," Harry continued.

"That would be Josh White," Randolph said. "He'd been with the hotel for years."

"Or, alternately, someone with a close friend in the hotel's maintenance department," Harry added.

"I'm not sure how Nicole Johnson was hired, but I can find that out," Randolph said quickly. He was clearly interested as to where Harry's tale was headed.

"Somehow, the thief came to learn that the medicine cabinet in each room was positioned back-to-back with the cabinet in the adjacent room. So—perhaps with the help of maintenance—they set up the cabinets in two specific rooms for easy removal," Harry continued.

He began to demonstrate his theory, using the salt and pepper shakers on the table. "For example, our guests are maneuvered into one of these special rooms—let's call it 1617. The cabinet in room 1615 has been outfitted to be easily pulled from the wall. This reveals the back of the adjacent cabinet. When the time comes, they simply push this cabinet into the bathroom of 1617, grabbing it before it falls and lowering it so that it rests on the top of the sink."

"And then they climb through the hole," Mark Kelly said. Glenn Randolph nodded along with him.

"Exactly," Harry said. He turned to Carol Hollinger. "You said two odd things which led me in this direction. The first was that toothpaste had been sprayed out of the tube."

"Yes," she said. "It was odd. Why would someone do that?"

"They did it unintentionally. When they lowered the heavy cabinet onto the counter, part of it landed on an open tube of toothpaste, ejecting the contents. Of course, the thief was behind the cabinet at this point and didn't notice. You also said the meager contents of the medicine cabinet where jumbled up, as if they had been ransacked like the rest of the room?"

"Yes, which was weird, because there were only a couple toiletries in the cabinet."

"Well, just like those cereal boxes that warn 'Contents May Have Shifted,' so too did the contents of that cabinet become jumbled up during the entrance and exit of our thief. The process of removing—and then replacing—the cabinet was enough to rearrange its contents topsy-turvy."

"So, in order to make this work, they needed control of which room a victim was assigned," Randolph said slowly.

"And they also had to be assured the adjacent room was unoccupied," Harry added. "Which points us heavily toward a clerk at the front desk. If my theory is correct, I wouldn't be surprised to learn they had set-up this configuration in more than one pair of rooms throughout the hotel, to give them options. And, of course, if successful, they wouldn't want to do the same trick twice in the same set of rooms."

"This should certainly be an easy thing to check out," Randolph said as he leaned back.

"Yes, I would imagine that the wall around the cabinet in the adjoining room would show some signs of tampering," Harry agreed. "Of course, if there is molding around the victim's cabinet, you'd be unlikely to detect any traces of the scheme."

"Well, this is certainly the most reasonable idea I've heard so far," Randolph said. "I know you magicians don't generally like to reveal how your tricks are done. Thanks for making an exception on this occasion."

"Always happy to assist the Four Horsemen of Criminal Apprehension," Harry said.

"And speaking of Apprehension, I think maybe the Department could return the favor by buying these gentlemen another round," Carol Hollinger suggested.

"Happy to do it," Glenn Randolph said with a grin. "As long as you approve the expense report."

"Consider it approved."

"Thanks folks," Harry said. "And Eli, as soon as you're done pouring the drinks, I'll show you what you're doing wrong with that iPhone card trick."

"I have a couple of notes as well," Abe added.

And so, after a quick trip to the bar, I returned to my customary position: learning at the feet of the masters, while the Four Horsemen of Criminal Apprehension returned to their drinks and their stories.

* * *

Two days later I received a short but enthusiastic phone call from Detective Randolph.

"Tell Harry his theory checked out," he said. "The medicine cabinet had been altered so it could be removed from the adjacent room. When we confronted Josh White, he immediately turned on his pal in maintenance. Apparently, they had hatched this plan several months ago and, like Harry suggested, were just waiting for the right opportunity."

"A smart pair," I said.

"Yes," Randolph agreed. "Although I doubt they knew they were re-imagining a magic trick from seventy odd years ago. Also, as Harry predicted, they had made adjustments to three different sets of adjacent rooms in the hotel, to increase their chances a room would be available on a moment's notice."

I told him I'd pass the good news along to Harry.

But before he let me go, Randolph then spent several minutes offering up his own theories on how I had pulled off the trick with the iPhone and the deck of cards. It was clear that, as Harry had suggested, he wouldn't be able to fully enjoy the trick until he knew how it was done.

Surprisingly, one of his ideas was actually pretty close to how I did it.

Of course, I'd never give him the satisfaction of admitting that.

THE $100 GIFT CERTIFICATE

I'm familiar with the sound made by the bell which hangs over our magic shop door.

Not in a Pavlovian sort of way, of course. For a sound to produce a repeatable physical effect (like Pavlov and the chime he rang to get his dogs to salivate), there must be a minimum number of repetitions for the stimulus to occur.

Our shop has simply never reached that necessary saturation point with the bell.

To put it another way, the bell has never needed to be replaced and likely never will.

Let me put a positive spin on this situation: on those rare occasions when a customer walks through that door, they're unlikely to be disturbed by other customers during their shopping experience.

Such was the case recently when a middle-aged man pushed the door open and stepped hesitantly into the shop. I glanced up at the sound of the bell. The man looked like he was coming in on a dare. His eyes darted around the space, as if someone might be lurking in the shadows, ready to pounce upon him.

Instead, all he got was me.

"Good morning," I said, my voice cracking from lack of use. "Can I help you find something today?"

This was my standard opening line with strangers, which were rare. Most people who came into Chicago Magic were either magicians or magic adjacent. Or they were lost or wanted change for the bus. But new customers weren't frequently seen on the premises; this fact alone explains all you need to know about how well—or not—I was running the business.

The gentleman didn't say anything, just approached the counter as he put a hand into his overcoat breast pocket. It seemed unlikely he was reaching for a gun. But try telling that to my flight or fight instinct, which to be honest is always heavily weighted toward flight. I inhaled quickly, mapping out an escape route in my head: Through the curtain, into the back of the shop, out the rear door, and run down the alley until I collapse.

The necessity for this short-range travel plan disappeared the moment his hand came out of his coat. He was holding a white, letter-sized envelope. He fumbled it open and pulled out the single sheet of paper within.

For a moment I thought he might be a process server and I was about to get a summons of some kind. To give you an idea of how bored I was at that moment, I found the prospect sort of exciting. He unfolded the sheet and handed it to me.

"Got this gift certificate from my co-workers," he said, his voice a flat monotone. "Need to use it."

I glanced down at the sheet he had handed me. It was indeed a gift certificate, in the amount of $100. The Chicago Magic logo was at the top of the sheet and my Uncle Harry's expansive signature was at the bottom. In between, a simple paragraph spelled out the specifications of the certificate, declaring the bearer was entitled to $100 worth of goods or services from Chicago Magic (applicable taxes not included).

Harry had come up with the idea of gift certificates years ago and had the sheets printed up in full color on a nice paper stock. Since then, I think we've sold less than a dozen. I'm not sure if this was due to lack of demand or poor marketing on our part. If history is any indicator, it was the latter.

"Fantastic," I said as I set the certificate down on the counter. "What exactly are you looking for?"

He glared back at me. He was maybe in his mid-forties, with a perpetual look on his face which suggested that something nearby had produced an unpleasant odor. Flecks of grey were evident in his otherwise dark hair.

"No idea," he said flatly. "Wasn't my idea in the first place. Don't really care for magic."

"This was a gift?" I said as I picked up the sheet again.

"Yes," he said. "Gift certificate. Didn't ask for it, didn't want it. Now I'm stuck with it."

"Well, if you really don't want it, you don't have to use it," I suggested. "You could return the certificate. It's not a standard procedure, but if you truly don't want it, I'd be happy to refund the money to you."

"Oh, that dog won't hunt," he said with a grim chuckle. "It's not my money, it's their money. Plus, they're going to ask what I got with it, and I'll need a plausible response. So, what do you have here that's plausible?"

I was stumped. I've been asked all manner of questions over the years about our products, but the level of their plausibility —or even the existence of their plausibility—had never been raised before.

"Um," I stammered as I tried to structure an answer. "Well, the store is divided into, I guess, what you would call several zones. The first and most general is well, magic tricks. Those might range from trick coins all the way up to large scale illusions, although the largest we have in the shop is an Okito

Checker Cabinet. Which I now remember we've sold. So, I guess that's not really an option."

He stared at me. I soldiered on.

"Then we have your magic supplies I guess you'd call them. Decks of cards, silks, balloons, magic wands, that sort of thing.

I might have been wrong, but I think he actually mumbled the word *harumph*.

"Anything else?" he asked.

"Well yes, I suppose so. We've got, um, your gag gifts."

"Gag gifts," he repeated.

"Sure, you know, your fake dog vomit, your squirting lapel flower, your joy buzzers."

He sniffed at the words. "Juvenile, that's simply juvenile."

I had to agree with him on that. And the thought of assembling $100 of those items was, in itself, a bit chilling. That purchase alone might empty the shelf entirely, which on the whole wasn't such a bad thought.

"Then we have, um, books and periodicals," I continued. "My uncle had a large catalog of books when he ran the shop and I've tried to keep up. So, there's everything from classics, like *The Expert at the Card Table*, right up to current releases, including Harry's own two-volume, career-spanning book. And we also have copies of lecture notes from a myriad of magicians over the years. And magazines, like *Genii, Magic Magazine, MUM, The Sphinx, The Jinx...*"

He peered over at the large bookcase which took up nearly one wall. "Those are just books about tricks? Magic tricks?"

"Mostly. Some books cover specific tricks and routines. Others discuss magic theory and the principles of magic. We also have a few biographies and autobiographies. In fact, I think we even have a signed copy of Sandy Marshall's book, *"Beating A Dead Horse: The Life and Times of Jay Marshall,"* if you're interested.

"Well, I'm not."

"I see." I scanned the room. I landed on the posters stacked in the corner. Some of them were framed and leaned up against the wall. Others were loose and assembled in a hanging file contraption that Harry had put together.

"If you're a fan of ephemera, we've got promotional posters and playbills for magicians and their shows, some of which date as far back as 100 years I think," I said, not sure why I was continuing on this fool's errand. "Magicians like Carter, Thurston, Blackstone Senior, and even a couple Houdini reprints. And somewhere I know Harry has an original Max Malini poster that he's probably willing to part with, but not for $100."

As I spoke, I realized I was long overdue to do a complete inventory of the store's products. At this rate, I thought, I could mark that task as done.

"Is that all?"

I searched my brain as I scanned the store again. There had to be something here I could unload on this guy.

There was nothing. Except me.

"Well, it's a bit below my standard rate, but I'd be happy to do a private show for you and your family and friends."

"Got no family."

I assumed his response implied he at least had friends, but I didn't want to press that point.

"A show for your co-workers, then? The people who gave you the gift certificate."

He shook his head. "No, I don't think so. Doesn't sound interesting."

At that moment, I could not agree with him more. Nothing seemed less interesting to me then performing for this fellow and the miscreants who had saddled him with this wholly unnecessary (and frankly, sort of mean-spirited) gift certificate.

I felt I had exhausted all avenues. And then one final thought occurred to me.

"Well, to fulfill the gift certificate, we could—if you're interested—use it to cover the cost of a lesson."

"A lesson?" he repeated. "You mean, like a magic lesson?"

I was going to make a crack about swimming lessons being an option as well but thought better of it.

He stared at me for a long moment. "Is that all you have?"

"Yes," I said. "I think it is literally all that I have."

He looked around the empty shop. "If that's all you've got."

"Terrific. When would you like to schedule it?"

"Now seems as good a time as any," he said. "Doesn't look like you have much else going on."

It was hard to argue with that.

"Yes, I suppose now's as good a time as any," I agreed.

I said he could call me Eli and he said I could call him Mr. Caldwell and we were off and running.

* * *

LESSONS WERE GENERALLY HELD in the back room, away from any possible prying eyes in the store. That of course wasn't currently a pressing issue, but I moved us to the table in the back more out of habit than anything.

"So, what are you looking for?" I asked as I gestured to one of the two chairs. "A little sleight of hand to do at a party? A card trick to amuse co-workers? Or something a little bit flashier?"

"I don't want anything flashy," he snapped back. "Not looking to draw attention to myself."

This was a challenge I had not faced in the few years I've been giving lessons. I'd never encountered someone who wanted to learn magic, yet at the same time did not want to draw attention to themselves.

"Okay," I said slowly. "Do you have a preference for card tricks, coin tricks, something with a phone or a Rubik's cube...?"

He stared back at me blankly as I listed these possible options.

"Don't like handling money," he said. "It's dirty. You don't know where it's been. And I don't care for that cube thing. Silly waste of time."

"Well that certainly helps narrow things down," I said, trying to put a smile in my voice. I think I failed. "Card tricks are pretty universal. It's easy to carry a deck of cards with you, and there are plenty of tricks we can do spontaneously."

"Not a big fan of spontaneity."

As my Uncle Harry was fond of saying, you could have knocked me over with a feather.

"So, what do you do for a living?" I asked, thinking this might open some doors to possible directions in which we might head, learning-wise.

"Insurance."

"Insurance, huh?"

"That's what I said."

"So, do you sell insurance, broker insurance, manage an insurance office," I said, quickly running out of possible job titles in the insurance business.

"I'm an actuary."

"Oh, a numbers guy," I said. "Perhaps something with a magic square, that can be fun."

"Numbers aren't toys to be played with."

He stared back at me. We engaged in a short game of eyeball chicken and then I caved and looked away.

"Okay," I said, stretching the word out to three syllables. It was pretty clear this was not going to be a long-term teacher/student relationship. I realized the smart thing to do would be to teach him a couple simple tricks and be done with it. It was not as if I was training him for a competitive spot at FISM. "Well, why don't I just show you a couple different kinds of tricks and we'll see if you spark to anything."

"Fine."

Seeing I wasn't likely to get a more enthusiastic response than that, I started with a simple version of The Ambitious Card, foregoing any theory and just jumping into the trick. I was about four moves in when he held up a finger to get my attention.

"Excuse me."

I stopped in mid-move.

"Yes?"

"Clearly that wasn't the top card you just showed me, although you said it was. Am I supposed to believe you on that point? I mean, is that part of the trick? Am I supposed to be aware of that deception?"

His questions, rattled off in his near monotone, lacked criticism or judgment of any kind. He was simply seeking clarification.

"Um, no, you're supposed to think the card I showed you was the top card on the deck."

"Well, I didn't think that. It was clear to me it wasn't the top card. Are you sure you're doing it right?"

Again, there was no judgement in his tone. Just a bare statement of facts.

I was reminded of an ongoing grammatical battle I'd waged with Uncle Harry over the years, as he labored to teach me the difference between *disinterested* and *uninterested*.

"They're simply not the same thing," Harry would grumble. "An *uninterested* person is bored or indifferent to what you're doing. A *disinterested* person is impartial; they have no stake in the outcome. A good referee would be disinterested."

While I had often struggled with the distinction, this encounter with Mr. Caldwell was vividly driving home the difference between the two words. He was absolutely *disinterested* and in the best way possible.

I considered offering the excuse that it had been a while since I'd done the trick (true enough) and that I was likely a little rusty (absolutely the truth), but I felt this wasn't the time for a defensive posture.

Instead, I backed up and performed that moment from the trick again. This repeated action received a slight shake of the head from my disinterested student. I did it three more times and finally got a blessed nod of approval.

"Yes, that time I believed it was the top card," he said.

"Fantastic," I said, relieved to have been given a passing grade. "Let's move on."

"Actually," Mr. Caldwell said, once again holding up a single finger. "There was an earlier moment which also failed to fool."

I tightened my grip on the cards, which was nowhere near the relaxed handling the trick required. "What would that be?"

"That moment when you said you were putting that card into the middle of the deck," Caldwell said. His tone suggested he'd discovered a minor but annoying accounting error in some banal audit. "It was clear to me the card wasn't being placed in the middle. Very clear, in fact."

This was a move which had famously and repeatedly fooled Houdini, I thought, but no matter. It wasn't getting past the eagle-eyed Mr. Caldwell.

"Let's run through it again, then," I said, working hard to take the rising tension out of my voice.

I performed that move four more times before finally getting the nod from my persnickety student. We continued the trick and he only had one more point of criticism ("If you wanted me to believe that you've actually cut the cards, I'm afraid you've fallen short of your goal."), which we were able to smooth over with only two repetitions of the action.

"So, that's the trick," I said once we'd finally reached the conclusion. It had felt like a very long journey indeed.

"Would it be possible to see it again?" Caldwell asked. This request was delivered in his same flat tone.

"You're in charge," I said.

I dutifully began the trick again from the top.

And, wouldn't you know it, the darnedest thing happened: As I went through the moves, I realized the trick was now, I don't know ... *better.* The small alterations I'd made based on his comments had actually improved the flow of the illusion. Not only was it more deceptive, but it also simply *felt* better in my hands.

I got to the end and couldn't help but smile. I looked up at Mr. Caldwell, who merely stared back at me blankly.

"Well, that's the trick," I finally said. I handed the cards to him. "Shall I start teaching you the moves?"

Caldwell scooted back, apparently repelled by the cards.

"Oh, goodness no," he said. "That's not for me. Show me something else."

I was surprised by this reaction, but probably shouldn't have been. It was pretty much in keeping with the attitude he'd had since he walked into the store. He clearly was not what you'd call a magic guy.

"Well, how about I show you something with coins? Of course, you wouldn't have to handle them," I quickly added.

"With that proviso, then certainly," he said, still registering zero excitement at the proposal.

"This is a variation on a coin matrix, made famous by David Roth," I said as I pulled four Kennedy half dollars from the coin purse in my pocket.

I recognized the trick was by no means suitable for a beginning magic student; however, it was something I'd been working on and it needed an audience. And, if nothing else, Mr. Caldwell was proving to be an ideal spectator for magic.

"For the sake of clarity, why don't I do the trick all the way through once," I suggested as I placed the four coins on a close up mat I'd added to the table. "And then we can address any comments or questions you might have."

"Fine," was all he said as he patiently waited for me to begin the routine.

I wouldn't call what I did next flawless, but it wasn't bad. I'd done Al Schneider's version of *Matrix* for years, using playing cards to cover the coins and reveal their various movements. But doing it barehanded was a new experience for me.

I got to the end of the routine and looked over at Mr. Caldwell. He stared down at the four coins, which were now all assembled in a small pile on one corner of the close-up mat. He looked up at me.

"I have some notes," was all he said.

This was the understatement to end all understatements.

There are maybe seven or eight moves in the short routine. He had thoughts on every single one of them, and even had some choice comments on several moments which occurred between the moves.

We went through the routine again, move by move. It was both a painful and productive experience. He questioned every step I took, asking why I did it this way and wouldn't it be better if I did it that way and isn't it obvious what you're doing there? And he did it all without a hint of criticism, an experience which was completely foreign to me.

I had learned just about everything I knew about magic from my uncle Harry, which I'd often joked was learning magic the hard way. He was not a warm and fuzzy teacher; Harry was quick with criticism and stingy with praise. Caldwell's approach wasn't the opposite, it was like the inverse. Like Uncle Harry but turned inside out.

After the routine had been thoroughly dissected, I ran it again. As I'd felt with the card trick, the coin piece felt crisper, sharper and, in a word, *better*. I executed the final move and looked up at Caldwell.

He stared back at me blankly. "Well, that works," was all he said.

"Yes, it does," I agreed. Since I knew he had no interest in learning the routine himself, I was frantically trying to think of another piece of mine which could benefit from this process. The problem wasn't landing on one; the problem was narrowing it down to just a single choice. I realized that just about everything I performed could benefit from the sort of precise examination he offered.

Before I could choose the next effect, I heard a muffled dinging. Caldwell reached into his coat pocket and pulled out his phone.

"That's ninety-minutes," he said as he switched off the alert. "That was what we agreed upon, right? Ninety minutes?"

"Give or take," I said quickly. "I'm not a stickler on hitting the exact time for lessons. Happy to go for another half hour or hour, if you'd like..."

But Caldwell was already standing. He slid the phone back into his pocket and straightened his suitcoat. "No, we agreed upon ninety minutes."

"I just don't want you to feel short-changed," I suggested, but he waved it away.

"I believe I've received the full value of the gift certificate," he said. "I can report back to my co-workers on that point with confidence." He looked around the cluttered backroom, orienting himself. "Egress is through that curtain, correct?"

"Yes, that's the way out."

I followed him through the curtain as he headed toward the

shop door. I grabbed the gift certificate off the counter as I passed it.

"If you want to use this again, feel free," I said as I handed the sheet toward him. He was already halfway to the door.

"No, thank you, that was fine," he said. "As I mentioned, I'm not really into magic and its accoutrements. But I appreciate your willingness to adjust the terms of your gift certificate to meet my needs."

"No problem," I said as I opened the door for him. The bell above it tinkled as the door swung open.

"Thank you and have a nice day," Caldwell said as he slipped through the door.

"No, thank *you*," I replied, but he was already gone. I let go of the knob and the door swung slowly shut.

I moved back to my original position behind the counter, scanning the gift certificate as I did. The sound of the bell tinkling over the door made me spin around in giddy anticipation.

But it was just Uncle Harry, stopping by before heading to the bar next door for lunch with the other Minneapolis Mystics.

"Expecting someone?" he said, surprised by my unexpected interest in his arrival.

"No, I just thought it was a magic student coming back, maybe he forgot something," I offered as I stepped behind the counter. I set the gift certificate down.

"You just had a lesson?"

"I did indeed," I said. "That might have been the best magic lesson ever."

Harry grinned at me. "I'm so glad you've started giving lessons," he said. "It's fun when the student becomes the teacher."

"And more fun when the teacher becomes the student," I said.

I didn't bother to look up to see his response to my comment. I already had my four silver half-dollars out and was practicing what Caldwell had revealed to me over the last hour or so.

In fact, I was so engrossed, I barely registered the sound of the bell when Harry left.

THE CRAZY MAN'S HANDCUFFS

"*It comes with the territory.*"

That phrase had always been my Uncle Harry's go-to retort. In his mind, it worked for virtually any of my whiny lamentations, from a teenage broken heart to complaints about the inevitable lines at the DMV. So, it wasn't surprising when his words echoed in my head as the persistent guest followed me to my next group of partygoers.

I had begun to think of him as my shadow, because he had latched onto me early in the evening. He seemed determined to witness each and every one of my close-up performances as I made my way through the large, brightly festooned ballroom. I had been hired for ninety minutes of walk-around magic and this middle-aged man seemed resolute in his self-imposed goal to see every single minute of it.

Walk-around magic, as it's been christened, doesn't require that you actually saunter while you perform. It instead means a magician moves from small group to small group—usually in a party situation—interrupting the flow of each gaggle's conversation with an offer to perform a bit of sleight of hand.

Some magicians hate it, some thrive on it. Most of us fall somewhere in the murky middle.

For myself, I have come to recognize its benefits, few as they may be. To begin with, in the right situation, it can pay quite well for an hour or two's worth of work.

It also doesn't require learning new material, as you essentially do the same few tricks for each group throughout your allotted time. As Uncle Harry was fond of telling me, a magician who knows six tricks can spend their entire career making a fine living only performing walk-around magic.

Besides the monetary benefit, the gig also allows the performer the paid opportunity to hone and perfect a trick in a short amount of time. If that's your goal.

As with most things, if you do the same magic trick twenty times in the course of an evening, by the end of that night you will have discovered all its shortcomings. And likely come up with a few workable solutions as well.

I wasn't using this gig as a chance to try out some new material—although, given the persistence of my constant companion, I was beginning to wish I had. Instead, I was relying on my fairly standard walk-around set, designed to get me into a small group, make an impression, and get out and onto the next group with minimal fuss.

I usually kicked things off with Richard Sanders' *Extreme Burn*, a great effect in which I transform five one-dollar bills into five one-hundred-dollar bills, all in less than the blink of an eye. It works on all occasions but is particularly effective in a room full of Type-A big-finance salespeople, which aptly described the crowd I was facing at this particular event. The room smelled of money and so it was the perfect trick to introduce myself to each high-powered cluster of partygoers.

Sticking with the theme of currency, I'd then move onto *Three-Fly*, a trick where I appear to make a coin 'fly' from one hand to the other. Among the many benefits of this trick is that it plays well at eye level; other tricks I'd used in the past required keeping my hands down by my waist, so the audience was essentially staring at my crotch throughout the routine. The change was a welcome one.

Finally, if they seemed minimally pleased with the performance and not itching to get rid of me, I'd wrap things up with a rubber band trick called *The Crazy Man's Handcuffs*. The trick is simplicity itself: An intertwined pair of rubber bands appear to melt through each other as they separate right before your eyes. It's a great way to wrap-up a short performance before moving on.

All in all, the gig was going well. In fact, the only insect in the evening's ointment was my newly acquired shadow, who appeared glued to my side as I did my short set for my latest small group of partygoers.

Don't get me wrong. It's not that I wasn't delighted with his enthusiasm.

It's not uncommon to pick up a groupie or two at these events; usually it's a middle-aged guy who had long ago abandoned the idea of becoming a performing magician in favor of getting a real job with a regular paycheck. Watching me perform often rekindled that spark of childhood wonder and fascination.

Alternatively, he could have been one of those people who simply could not rest until he figured out how a trick was accomplished. Thus, the need for multiple viewings.

He was reminding me of a ploy often employed by Uncle Harry. On more than one occasion at a magic convention, Harry had been approached by a younger magician who wanted to demonstrate his or her latest effect to the master himself.

If Harry could spot how the trick worked, he'd usually offer some heartfelt praise and perhaps a word or two of advice. However, if Harry couldn't immediately figure out how it was done, he'd say something along the lines of, *"Oh, my. You know who would love that?"* He'd then say the name of another well-known magician and drag the kid across the room to perform it for this new audience.

If Harry could figure out the trick on this second viewing, he'd call it a day. If not, once again he'd say, *"You know who needs to see this trick?"* For a second time, they'd cross the room for an impromptu performance for this new victim. Usually by the fourth or fifth repetition of the routine, Harry would figure out the method and release the unsuspecting magician back into the wild.

I was getting that same, sneaking suspicion about my stalker.

I thanked the latest small group and moved away from the cluster while I glanced at my watch. My ninety minutes was just about done, so I scanned the ballroom to see if I could catch sight of the Event Planner. My contract requires payment at the end of the gig, and the notion of grabbing my check and heading home was utmost in my mind. For a delightful moment, I'd forgotten about my new best friend. And then, for the first time that night, I heard him speak.

"What's that last trick called?"

I turned. He was, as always, just inches away. "Excuse me?"

"The trick with the rubber bands. What's that called?"

I stopped and considered his simple and direct question.

In my early days, I would have immediately offered up the name of the effect. But with the emergence of smart phones and Google, supplying a trick's name was essentially the same thing as telling him how the trick was done. A two-second search would provide him a plethora of videos revealing the secret behind the effect.

My admittedly lame solution was to offer quickly made-up names for the tricks, to throw them off the scent. Like, "That's

'*The Preminger Effect, with an Otto Stinger,*'" I'd say. Or, "That one is called '*Hawks & Handsaws.*'"

Of course, I knew full well that—at best—I was merely slowing them down. If they really wanted the solution, the Internet was more than willing to provide.

However, it was the end of the night and he'd seen the rubber band trick a minimum of twelve times, so what did it matter?

"When Arthur Setterington came up with it, he called it '*Getaway,*'" I began. "Then Herb Zarrow did some work on it. Lou Tannen put that version in *Tarbell 7*, which Harry Lorayne wrote."

I was, from force of habit, providing him a longer chain of ownership than he'd probably wanted. "However," I continued. "The version I do is pretty close to the one Michael Ammar was famous for, which Daryl nicknamed '*The Crazy Man's Handcuffs.*' It doesn't require anything special, just two normal rubber bands. I'm sure you can find tons of video instructions for it on-line."

He was nodding along with my recitation, but I got the sense he wasn't really listening.

"Here, you can have these," I said as I pulled two rubber bands from my pocket. "We'll call it a starter kit."

He took the bands from me but didn't look at them. He was staring blankly off into the distance. He turned to me suddenly, his eyes now sharp and focused.

"I want to hire you," he said.

"Sure thing," I said as I reached for a card. "Are you looking for a performance or are you interested in magic lessons?"

"No," he said with a quick shake of his head. "I need you to help me kill someone."

* * *

FROM HAVING WORKED that hotel frequently in the past, I knew two things about its lobby bar: If an open-bar event was going on in the ballroom, the lobby's tavern would be just about vacant.

But regardless of the number of occupants, instead of the traditional bowl of peanuts or beer nuts at each table, this establishment set out bowls of whole, salted cashews.

On every table.

It was like heaven with Muzak.

With those two thoughts in mind, I found us a table in the back. We placed our drink order with a bored server, who was clearly surprised to see any patrons at all. As he ordered his vodka gimlet, I took a closer look at my shadow.

He was definitely middle-aged, although I'd found my precise definition of that term was getting murkier the older I got. But he was clearly somewhere in that no-man's land between forty and fifty, with a hairline that was receding in direct proportion to his expanding waistline. His face was headed toward doughy, but the remnants of a sharp chin and cheekbones were still visible. He wore a good suit, but it was nowhere near as sharp (or expensive) as most of the others I'd seen in the ballroom we'd just left.

Once the server had departed, he turned to me. "Thanks for sticking around and not running for the nearest exit," he said with a chuckle. "Despite my creepy sales pitch."

"It was certainly an attention-grabber," I agreed. "Dave, was it?"

He nodded. "Yep, Dave."

"And you're writing a story?"

He shrugged. "Well, I'm trying to."

"And you want me to help you kill someone? In the story?" I was repeating back his hurried explanation from our ballroom conversation, to clarify his intentions.

"I'd love to get your thoughts." He glanced down at the

bowl of cashews in front of us, grabbed one and then pushed the bowl away. It was his third trip to the dish since we'd sat down. "Got to cool it on these things," he said.

I re-directed the bowl's location to my side of the table and grabbed a couple cashews in the process. "What's the story about?"

The question gave him pause and he took it, considering his words carefully.

"I'm still trying to sort it out in my head," he said finally. "You see, I've always wanted to start writing fiction, but one thing or another—work, usually—has gotten in my way. But I made a New Year's resolution to make some big changes, and so far I'm making at least a little progress. But then I hit a wall and need some help getting over it."

I nodded and glanced down at the cashew bowl, quickly calculating how soon it would be depleted based on my current rate of cashew consumption. I looked around casually and was happy to spot a nearly full bowl just out of my reach at the next table. I made a mental note of its existence.

"It's a thriller, kind of a murder thing," Dave continued. "About a guy who kills his wife and the young cop who tries to figure it out. But, you know, literary in a way. Suburban angst, mid-life crisis, that sort of thing."

"Like John Cheever meets John Sanford?"

He nodded quickly, although I wasn't convinced he'd fully understood the analogy. "Exactly. But I'm having trouble with the murder. I mean, coming up with a good one. Because, in the end, I want my guy to get away with it."

"Well, if you're looking for advice on police procedure," I began, "my ex-wife is an Assistant District Attorney. And her husband is a Homicide detective. He's not particularly chatty, but he does know his stuff. I could hook you up with them for some inside information—"

Dave shook his head. "No, no. I mean, thanks, but no," he

said quickly. "I thought you, as a magician, might have some clever notions, something outside the box. It occurred to me when you did that trick with the rubber bands."

"*The Crazy Man's Handcuffs.*"

"Right," he nodded. "I mean, I love the metaphor: Two objects, seemingly joined together. Interwoven. Entangled. And then, due to some unseen force, the bond between them seems to just melt away. And they're no longer together. Two completely separate entities. As metaphors go, that's a pretty good description of my situation. In the story," he quickly added.

The server arrived with our drinks and we were silent for a few moments as she arranged the glasses in front of us. For her final move, she took the nearly depleted cashew bowl from in front of me and swapped in the full one from the next table. I mentally doubled her tip.

"Here's the situation," Dave said once the server had moved away. "This guy's been married since high school, because they got pregnant. A common trope, I know. Then another kid and another. He's working in an industry he despises, has gotten about as far up the ladder as he's likely to get. He hates his life, he's feeling stuck. Trapped really," he added as he took a deep sip from his glass.

"And murder is his only way out?"

He shrugged. "In his mind, yes. He has come to learn that his wife is really a terrible, terrible person. Constant abuse. Belittling him. She would never give him the satisfaction of a divorce. Plus, there's a hefty life insurance policy."

"People have killed for less," I agreed.

"You bet. But I want something foolproof," he continued, looking down at the drink in his hand. "Foolproof," he repeated, as much to me as to himself.

"Well, as my pal Jamy Ian Swiss used to say, nothing is foolproof, because fools can be very determined." But I'm not sure he heard this.

"He's smarter than the police," he said quietly. "He knows that. And the murder is his way of proving it. I mean, they might suspect he did it, but they can never, ever prove it."

We sat silently for several moments as he continued to stare down at the table. I could feel the tension in his shoulders and watched as the muscles in his jaw clenched and unclenched.

"What have you come up with so far?" I finally asked, although my mind had moved onto other more pressing concerns. I was thinking about how I could slip my phone out of my pocket and discretely start the 'record' function. But I wasn't sure how I might accomplish that without drawing attention to the action. A bit of misdirection was required. And I was coming up empty.

Immediately I heard my uncle Harry's voice in my head: *"Do it on the off-beat."* I understood, in theory, what he meant. However, I wasn't sure where the off-beat—or, for that matter, the on-beat—was in this unique situation.

The Harry voice in my head must have sensed my confusion, because he continued: *"Okay, then. Let the big action cover the little action."*

Was that the concept? Or was it *"Let the little action cover the big action?"* Both—and neither—were making sense to me at the moment. I began to lean toward the second version, and then I hit another roadblock: What would constitute a big action in this situation?

As if to answer me, the server picked that moment to walk past.

"Another of the same," I said with a gesture toward my nearly full glass as I waved her over. "And I'd like to start a tab."

As I spoke, I reached into my coat pocket and removed my wallet, slipping out the phone in the same fluid action. "How about you?" I asked my companion, turning to him as I handed a credit card to the server. As I did that, I set the wallet—with the phone underneath it—on the table to my left, just out of Dave's line of sight.

My deceptive move went unnoticed, because he shook his head without even looking up. The server nodded and continued on her way. Using my wallet as cover, I tried to start the recording function on the phone but was having trouble remembering the sequence of steps required to activate the little-used app.

"What was your question?" He looked up, clearly deep in his own thoughts.

"What methods have you considered so far?" I asked as my fingers slid blindly across the phone's smooth face.

"Oh, all kinds of crazy things," Dave said. "I even had one idea where he arranges things so it appears to the police that her lover had killed her. And that the lover has gone to great lengths to frame my guy for the crime. I liked that: Framing the lover so it looks like he's framing me. My guy."

"She has a lover?"

He nodded. "Multiple lovers, over the years. She isn't shy about it. Like I said, she's a horrible person. But that idea was just too darned convoluted."

"Simple is hard," I agreed, once again hearing Harry's voice from throughout the years, chiding me over my handling of one trick or the other.

"*No, no,*" he would say, clearly exasperated. "*Easy is not the same as simple. Any hack can make a trick easy, but to make it truly simple—to shape its elements so they're at their most direct and straightforward—that can take even the most brilliant magician years to achieve.*"

"It's too bad," he said. "I would love to be able to frame the lover, so that he takes the fall."

"Killing two birds, as it were."

"That would be great." He grinned for the first time, really seeming excited by this notion. "Just great."

I was getting nowhere with the app and was suddenly struck with an idea.

"Oh," I said a little too brightly. "I think I just got a text. Excuse me."

I wasn't likely to win an Academy Award, but he seemed to believe that I had indeed just that moment received a message. I held my phone so he couldn't see the screen, performing a mix of terrible mime and actual swiping to make it look like I was responding to a text. Finally, with more effort than I'd anticipated, I got the recording app up and running.

"Crisis averted," I said, again a bit too brightly as I set the phone back on the table, face down. I gave it a slight nudge, so that its microphone was pointed in Dave's direction. "So, your ideal scenario would be to frame her lover for the murder?"

He nodded, still smiling at the notion. Realizing that nodding would not play well on the recording, I continued.

"Have you taken any steps or formed any plans?" I asked, then added quickly. "I mean, in the story?"

He shook his head as his smile disappeared. "The details are the hard part."

"That's true in magic as much as fiction," I agreed.

"So how do you do it?" he asked, turning toward me. "How do you fool people, make them think one thing is happening when something else is actually at work?"

"That's a big question," I said slowly. "That might be the biggest question in magic, with all kinds of answers. Most of the time, the audience does half the work for you. Or more, even."

"How do you mean?"

"Well, one common fallacy is that the show starts when the magician comes on-stage. In reality, he or she may have done a ton of pre-show work, so that by the time the curtain opens, a lot of the heavy lifting has already taken place."

"So, the murder could start before it actually starts," he said as he turned and looked off into the distance.

"Then there's the concept of dual-reality: the audience thinks one thing is going on, while your volunteer onstage is having a wholly different experience."

He seemed to still be processing the previous idea. He looked over at me.

"You mean, it looks like one thing is happening to one group, while others are experiencing something else?" he repeated, saying the words slowly as he considered the concept.

"That's the idea," I said. "And then, don't discount the use of stooges."

"Moe and Curly and the other one?" He was clearly mystified at what appeared to be an unannounced shift in the direction of our conversation.

"No, stooges from the audience. Plants. People you've worked with ahead of time to help sell an effect. To the audience, they don't appear to be involved in the magic. But it couldn't happen without them."

"Do magicians use a lot of stooges?"

I shook my head. "In reality, hardly ever."

Although I could have named a few magicians who employ nearly an army of stooges, they were the exception to the rule and not germane to our discussion. Then it occurred to me that I really should be the one making Dave talk, if capturing evidence was my intention.

"So, what other ideas have you already vetoed?" I took a sip of my drink, gesturing that the floor was his.

As Dave quickly listed off some ideas he'd come up with and rejected, I looked down at the phone, hoping the app was silently doing its job. At the same time, I was also wondering if what I was doing was strictly legal.

I couldn't help think back to the multiple conversations I'd had on this very topic with my ex-wife while we were married. She was always railing about this recording or that recording being deemed inadmissible at the last minute, which resulted in her case collapsing. Her monologues on the topic were long and profane.

While I had sharp memories of the tone of these speeches, I was wishing I had listened a little closer to the finer points of her arguments. The fact was, I really wasn't sure if what I was doing was going to help put Dave in jail ... or help him avoid it.

I snapped back to attention when it was clear he had finished his litany.

"In short," he concluded. "All my ideas have literally been done to death and would be spotted in an instant by even the dimmest of detectives."

"New ideas are rare," I began, not sure where I was headed. Then, once again, Uncle Harry's voice echoed in my brain and offered a direction.

"My uncle Harry is a real old pro in the magic world," I said. "Been everywhere, done everything. And he's always said that in magic, the best way to hide a brilliant idea is to put it in a book. No magician would ever think to look for it there.

"The truth is, one of the best ways to come up with a smart idea is to take an old idea and make it your own. Give it a new spin, add a different, unique dimension," I continued. "There are tons of fantastic ideas out there; people are just too lazy to search them out. So maybe you could find something in one of the thousands of true crime novels out there. Or on Netflix; they seem to have no shortage of documentaries about spouses killing each other."

Dave shook his head. "I appreciate the concept," he said. "But those books and documentaries are all focused on the people who got caught. That's not what I'm looking for."

I could see his point. "It does make you wonder why they

don't produce a few shows on the people who got away with murder, if only to balance the scales," I suggested.

"I wish."

I considered my own, limited history of murder. In all the cases my ex-wife had been involved in—and the few I'd had even a slight connection with—ultimately the killer was captured.

And then I remembered one possible exception.

"There was one case," I began as I thought back on the circumstances. "I thought the killer was pretty clever, but they fell just short of the mark, so to speak. I mean, they were caught. But they didn't have to be."

This statement clearly sparked Dave's interest, and he turned to face me expectantly. The server arrived at that moment with my wholly unnecessary second drink, setting it next to the nearly full one in front of me. She silently handed back my credit card before moving on. I sensed judgement in her body language. Once she was out of earshot, I continued.

"The method they employed was clever," I said quietly. "They used the victim's sleep apnea machine. They put poison in with the water for the device's humidifier chamber. As it heated up, the poison melted and was inhaled by the victim while he slept."

"And that worked?"

"Like a charm," I said. "The victim appeared to have died in his sleep, because the poison stopped his heart. The reason they got caught was that the killer used a common poison—like cyanide or strychnine or something—which was easily detected during the autopsy. But I remember one of the cops telling me they would have gotten away with it, if only they'd been smart enough to use a non-detectable poison."

"So that was their mistake," Dave said as he considered the scenario I'd presented. "They just picked the wrong kind of poison. Otherwise, they would have gotten away with it?"

I shrugged. "That's what the detective said."

"Poison. In her damned sleep apnea machine," he repeated. "That would work nicely."

I suddenly realized I might have gone too far in my efforts to keep our conversation rolling. "Of course," I said, back peddling quickly, "with today's forensics, there's probably no such thing as an undetectable poison."

"Oh, I'm sure there's something out there, somewhere," Dave mumbled. I could tell the wheels were turning in his brain. I was frantically trying to think of a way to reverse that process. He finished his drink quickly as he reached into his coat pocket. He pulled out his phone and glanced at it.

"Oh, that's my ride," he said as he made some quick swipes and taps on the small screen. Either he was a better actor than me or he was actually responding to a real text.

"So, anyway, Dave, we should stay in touch, in case I come up with more ideas," I began, but he cut me off.

"Did I say my name was Dave?" he said. He appeared to be grinning as he pushed himself back from the table.

"I'm pretty sure you did," I said. But my confidence in that detail was suddenly not so strong.

"Interesting choice," he said. "Almost Freudian."

"So, are you heading back to the event? In the ballroom?" I continued, trying to sound as casual as possible.

He seemed puzzled by this suggestion.

"Oh, that cocktail party?" He shook his head and smiled. "No, I just wandered in there. Classic interloper, that's me. I'm not even staying at this hotel. Anyway, it was great talking to you. What do I owe you for the drink?"

I waved that notion away. "I'd really love to chat more," I said quickly, trying to think of a way—any way—to keep him talking so I could gather more information about him and his intended victim.

"No, I think we're good," he said. "Great trick, by the way.

The thing with the rubber bands. Really clean. What did you call it again?"

"*The Crazy Man's Handcuffs*," I sputtered.

I couldn't believe what was happening. I'd sat down for a drink with a sociopath and stupidly given him a foolproof method for murdering his wife and getting away with it. Not only was he a monster, but I was practically an accomplice.

"See you around."

He headed toward the door and I struggled to my feet to follow him, but the server was once again in front of me. She was holding a receipt and a pen. I quickly signed it and took a couple precious seconds to calculate a reasonable tip, before handing it back to her and racing toward the door. I made it about ten feet and then hurried back to grab my wallet and my phone.

The bar emptied out into the hotel's main lobby, which was bustling even at this late hour. The event must have wrapped up, as partygoers were pouring through the lobby, either heading toward the bar or the valet stand.

I scanned the large space, looking for any sign of my drinking companion, but he had somehow vanished. I looked toward the line at the valet stand on the other side of the revolving doors, but he didn't appear to be part of that growing queue. I looked toward the ballroom, but he wasn't in sight.

"Are you looking for someone?" The voice was resonant and reassuring. I turned to see a handsome black man, maybe in his fifties. He was standing a few feet away, his phone in his hand.

"Um, sort of," I stammered. "I was just having a drink. With a guy. In the bar. And now I can't find him."

"I seem to have lost my date as well," he said with a smile. He looked me over again. "Say, aren't you the magician who was performing at the party?"

I nodded while I continued to scan the room. "Yes, that was me."

"Let me take a guess: was this drinking companion of yours looking for a way to kill his wife?"

His words stopped me cold. I turned to him, surprised to see he was still smiling.

"He might have been," I offered.

"Sorry about that," he said. He shook his head slowly. "I really can't take him anywhere."

"Where were you taking him?" Suddenly this new conversation was as confusing as the last one.

"It's our twenty-fifth anniversary, and he was nice enough to be willing to spend it here, while I put in an appearance at this work event," he said with a nod toward the ballroom. I followed his gaze and then turned back to him.

"So, he's not killing his wife?" I offered.

He shook his head. "Back in the day, I dated all kinds of people," he said. "Even a couple of magicians," he added with a grin. "And I can tell you this: Magicians may be weird. But writers are weirder."

"So, he really is writing a story..." I began, my words trailing off.

"And looking for a foolproof murder scheme?" he said, completing my thought. "Yes, he is. God help us if the authorities ever go through our search history. No jury in the world would acquit."

"He really sucked me in."

"Good writers do that," he offered. "And speak of the devil. Here he is now."

I turned to see Dave—or whatever his name might be—headed toward us.

"Sorry, had to visit the little writer's room before the ride home," he said, greeting his partner with a quick kiss on the cheek. He turned to me. "And thanks again for the drink. And the ideas. I think I've really got a handle on this one now."

"Glad to be of service," I said. I realized my phone was still in my hand and that the app was still running. I didn't care anymore.

"Our Uber is waiting for us," his partner said, gently nudging him toward the revolving doors. "Nice meeting you," he said over his shoulder.

Dave was still bubbling over with excitement. "I think, with his help, I've really cracked it," he said. And then they disappeared into the crowd heading out the door.

I looked down at my phone. The recording app was showing a little timecode window informing me that it had been twenty-two minutes since I had started my recording. I hit the STOP button and then pushed the file into the trash.

I stood there for a long moment as people pushed past me. My adrenaline was still pumping.

And then, as I slowly returned to reality, I realized that in all the commotion I hadn't tracked down the Event Planner. She still held my check for my ninety-minutes of work. I began to move toward the ballroom, like a salmon heading upstream.

I had to agree with the man. Magicians may be weird, I thought.

But writers are weirder.

THE SECONDARY CONVINCER

"I'm sorry. Were you doing a magic trick or something?"

I'd like to say this was the first time I'd ever received that response to a performance, but I'd be lying. There were just the two of us hanging out at the bar—him seated in front of it, me working behind it. And since I was holding a deck of cards, I had made the foolish assumption that I was, in fact, doing a trick.

"No, I'm just goofing around," I lied. "Practicing, I guess."

I thought briefly about that old adage: if a tree falls on a magician in a forest doing a trick, and the only other person there isn't paying attention, was it actually a trick?

Okay, I know that isn't truly an old adage. But it probably should be.

The customer picked up his drink and noticed a playing card stuck to the bottom of the glass. He peeled it off. "Is this part of the trick?"

"Well, not anymore," I said.

I took the card from him and, still in practice mode, tried a couple of moves, finally making the card seem to disappear.

The effect was pretty clunky. Perhaps practicing wasn't such a bad idea.

"I wish you could make me disappear just as easily," he said before taking another long sip from his drink.

My lone customer sitting at the bar, Mark Kelly, had recently become something of a regular. For reasons I didn't completely understand, the watering hole had started attracting police types. Kelly wasn't strictly in law enforcement but considered himself law enforcement adjacent: He was a former cop who was now a freelance investigator for big insurance companies.

He may have been in-shape during his cop days, but they were long behind him now. He was beefy headed toward burly, with a round face and big, doughy hands. Even though it was cool in the bar, he always looked a little moist. I imagined his cholesterol numbers and blood pressure figures were nothing to write home about.

Kelly glanced at his watch, downed the rest of his drink and pushed the glass toward me. "More of the same, please."

"You keep looking at your watch." I set down the deck of cards and picked up the glass. "Are you supposed to be somewhere?"

He shook his head. "In thirty-five minutes, I have to call my client and give him some bad news. He has to make a $350,000 payout."

"Yikes," I said.

"Yikes in spades," Kelly replied. "He's not going to be happy about it. Despite their marketing which may suggest otherwise, insurance companies don't like writing out checks. Regardless of the size. In fact, I get the sense this particular client would prefer not to even *own* a checkbook."

I placed the new drink in front of him and he took a quick sip. "This is not the kind of news anyone likes to receive or deliver. And I have this sick feeling he may be inclined to blame the messenger. I know I would. So, needless to say, I'm not looking forward to calling in my report."

"At least you don't have to do it in person," I offered.

"A small blessing," he said with a sigh. "The thing is, I've done my due diligence. In my heart, I know the claimant did something sneaky; I just can't prove it."

"That's a common issue with magic tricks as well," I said. I attempted a quick one-handed cut with the deck of cards. Yes, more practice was definitely in my future. "Sometimes there's a point in the trick where the audience *knows* you did something sneaky. They can sense it. They just don't know exactly what it was."

"Yep, that's what I'm up against. This guy did something. I just don't know what it was. But everything fell into place too neatly."

"It's too perfect."

He nodded. "Exactly, it's too perfect."

"And that's why you don't believe it. Because it's too perfect."

He nodded again.

"We have the same thing in magic," I said. "Which we call, not so surprisingly, the Too Perfect theory."

"Oh heavens, we're not talking about that old chestnut again, are we?" This came from my uncle Harry, who had tottered over from the far corner for a refill on his ginger ale.

"It's a questionable theory to some," he continued as he set his empty glass on the bar. "To others, it's a stone-cold fact. And then there's a happy majority who never even think about it. Put me in that latter camp, thank you very much."

"I was just referencing it in connection to a case he's working on," I explained.

I added ice to the empty glass and then refilled it with ginger ale, which was Harry's afternoon drink of choice. Although, unbeknownst to him, he was now getting *diet* ginger ale, on secret instruction from his wife. Mercifully, Harry hadn't appeared to recognize the difference. If he did, I knew I'd never hear the end of it.

"So, what's *too perfect* about this case you're working on?" Harry said as he pulled himself up on a stool. "Or is it all terribly hush-hush and on a need-to-know basis?"

Kelly shook his head. "It's been in all the papers and all over the Internet. I mean, when you discover you own artwork painted by Adolf Hitler, people tend to sit up and take notice."

I set Harry's glass in front of him on the bar, but he was too caught up in this new twist to even notice.

"I hadn't heard anything about this," he said. "Sounds fascinating. Tell me more."

* * *

THE CASE MARK KELLY outlined for us over the next few minutes had caused a small sensation when it broke.

A local art dealer, The TR Gallery, had been bequeathed a number of old paintings (and a sizable financial contribution) by a recently deceased wealthy patron. The bequest came with one proviso: the gallery needed to produce a special exhibition featuring all the pieces in the collection. This they had dutifully done, only to discover—via an eagle-eyed and knowledgeable patron—that one of the pieces was likely the work of the infamous former German Chancellor.

Experts were summoned, tests were performed, and it quickly became evident the painting was in fact authentic. The gallery was showing a picture brushed by Adolf Hitler himself.

"Once the legitimacy of the painting had been established by the experts," Kelly continued, "The owner did a smart thing, PR-wise: he declared the gallery would never sell the painting. Instead, once this exhibition was closed, they would warehouse the piece, preserving it, but keeping it from the public eye. It would be available for academic study, but the gallery would not profit from it in any manner."

"Smart move," I agreed.

"Right," Kelly said with a shake of his head. "Then, for good measure, he went ahead and insured it for $350,000."

Harry raised an eyebrow at this information. "Is it worth $350,000?"

"Undoubtedly, to someone," Kelly said. "Of course, the gallery owner doesn't want to be the fellow who sells it. Because then that's how his gallery is labeled forever: the place that sells Hitler paintings."

"Not good for their brand, I would imagine," Harry mumbled.

"Not good for anyone's brand," I agreed. "But it never came to that, did it?"

Kelly shook his head. "Before the exhibition closed, a couple of fanatics broke into the gallery one night and destroyed the painting."

"And now the gallery owner is due a check for $350,000?"

"Well, he thinks he is," Kelly said. "Me, I'm not so sure."

"How do you mean *destroyed*?" Harry asked. He clearly had lost interest in his refreshed ginger ale. I slid a coaster under the glass, which had begun to perspire as much as Kelly. "Do you know what the burglars actually did?"

"We know *exactly* what they did, because they videotaped it and posted it on-line." Kelly pulled out his phone as he continued. "Ironically, the video itself has gotten close to 350,000 hits so far."

He made a couple quick swipes across the face of the phone and then turned it toward us.

The video was silent, but the actions spoke for themselves. It began on what I assumed was the Hitler painting: A pleasant watercolor of a simple, pastural scene.

A masked figure entered the shot and removed the framed

artwork from the wall. He (or she—the mask and a bulky jump-suit made identification impossible) then carefully removed the painting from its frame. The frame was tossed aside as the camera followed the burglar across the dark gallery toward a table, where a paper shredder had been set up. The burglar switched on the machine and carefully fed the small painting into the slot on the top of the device. The camera panned down as the shredded pieces of the canvas formed a small pile on the floor.

The masked burglar then removed a bottle from their pocket and poured the contents on the pile. Then they lit a match and tossed it on the floor. The small shredded heap burst into an immediate blaze, sending a spray of flames a couple feet into the air.

The camera held on the burning mound for several moments and then suddenly went black.

Mark Kelly spun the screen around, shut off the app and returned the phone to his pocket.

"Before you ask, yes, we did tests on the video and the ashes," he said. "It's not a deep fake—there are no edits in the video. What you see is what happened. And the remains, the ashes, are consistent with a canvas from that era."

"Interesting," I said. I looked over at Harry, who was stroking his beard. I was pretty sure his train of thought was heading in the same direction as mine. "So, from the gallery owner's perspective, this event—the break-in, the shredding, the burning—was the best thing that could have happened, right?"

Kelly nodded. "Absolutely. He's no longer stigmatized for owning the painting, yet he also is now the happy recipient of a check for $350,000. Or will be, after I make that call."

"Of course," Harry offered, "if he's the unscrupulous type and the painting hadn't *actually* been destroyed, he could go ahead and sell it on the black market and make an additional

$350,000—or more—without the stigma of being the guy who sells Hitler paintings."

"He sure could," Kelly said.

Harry sat quietly for a few moments and then looked down at the bar. He seemed surprised to see his glass of ginger ale in front of him. He looked up at me.

"Well, to begin with, that's an odd thing, isn't it? That secondary convincer, I mean."

I nodded. "That's the first thing I thought of."

"The secondary what?" Kelly said.

"The convincer," I explained. "It's a term we use in magic. It's the steps you add—during a magic trick—to remove from the audience's mind all the different ways the trick could have been done."

"You're closing doors to possible solutions as you perform the illusion," Harry added.

"Exactly. So, once you've eliminated all those options, the only conclusion they can come to is that what you did was actual magic."

"I'm not sure I follow," Kelly said.

I picked up the deck of cards. "Well for example, as I'm doing a card trick, I may turn the deck in such a way that you can see that all the cards are different. I don't draw any attention to this, but it convinces you it's a real deck and that all the cards aren't the same."

"So, the audience member isn't thinking, 'Well, the deck consists of nothing but the King of Diamonds. That's how he knew my card,'" Harry added.

"Then at a key point, I'll turn over both hands or gesture or something, so you can see that I haven't palmed a card."

"You're just knocking down possible explanations like dominoes in a line," Harry said.

"Exactly. I haven't drawn any attention to the fact, but I've demonstrated the way you thought the trick was being done isn't the way it's being done. I've closed off that method. It's a convincer."

"A good magic trick is loaded with convincers, each one destroying another option in your mind," Harry said. He took a quick sip of his ginger ale. I was surprised and relieved he couldn't distinguish diet from the full-strength version. "Convincers aren't consciously registered by the audience members, but they subtly lead them toward an inevitable conclusion: they've just seen actual magic."

"Okay," Kelly said slowly. "But how does that relate to this video and the destruction of the painting?"

"Well, your burglars used two convincers when they only needed one to make us believe they had destroyed the painting," I explained. "They shredded the painting and they burned it. What's the point of that?"

"Exactly," Harry said. "It doesn't make sense until you recognize the second convincer isn't simply a repeat of the first one. We don't need that again. We've seen the painting shredded. It's been destroyed. Why destroy it a second time?"

"What the second convincer was designed to do," I said, "was to take the focus off the shredder and put it back on the painting."

"Yes. They don't want us thinking about that darned shredder anymore," Harry added. "Forget about it, just focus on the destroyed painting. Focus on the fire."

"Look, look there's a big, bright, shiny fire," I said.

"In reality, what they did doesn't require a secondary convincer," Harry grumbled. "In fact, its very existence puts the validity of the first convincer—i.e., the shredder—in question. If the shredder destroyed the painting, why are we destroying it again? A convincer is designed to eliminate doubt, not feed it." He shook his head as he took another sip from his glass. "In my mind, this was a very sloppy trick indeed."

"So, you think it was a trick?" Kelly said. His face bright-ened for the first time since he'd sat down at the bar.

"Oh, it was absolutely a trick," Harry said

"Then how was it done?"

* * *

HARRY TOOK that moment to mention, not for the first time, that the bar stools weren't merely uncomfortable but "bordered on medieval torture devices." Since it appeared this conversation might be a long one, I moved our discussion to one of the many empty tables, of which the bar had no shortage.

Once we were settled in, Harry picked up where we'd left off at the bar.

"Offhand, I could think of maybe four or five ways to do it. However, if we believe in Occam's razor, and I certainly do, then the simplest answer is probably the right one." Harry turned to me. "Are you thinking what I'm thinking?"

"Not always, but in this case, I think yes," I said. "The counterfeit bill detector."

Harry nodded. "Exactly. Do we still sell them?"

I thought about this for a long moment, mentally scanning the magic shop next door and its gag and gift corner. "I think so," I said without confidence. "Let me go check."

Even though I'd just settled into a somewhat comfortable chair, I once again jumped up and headed across the room.

In the early days of owning the bar, I'd find myself making several trips a day between this space and the magic shop next door. That was fine during the summer, but once the hard reality of the Minnesota winter hit, I knew I needed another solution. I needed a door between the bar and the magic store.

Once I'd announced that decision, there had been a lot of discussion about the nature of that egress. Harry wanted a sliding bookcase that would require a magic word to open, ala

The Magic Castle. Nathan, the kids' magician who basically ran the magic shop while I was managing the bar, said he preferred an optical illusion of some kind. "One of those 3D murals. Something that delights the mind," he had said.

While I was all for delighting the mind, I was also stuck in the actual, physical world. There was only one spot on the wall that would work for a door on this side, and also match up on the other side. There wasn't room for a sliding bookcase, or some sort of full-scale illusion. There was space, just barely, for a standard, 36-inch door.

Which is what I had installed.

"It's not fancy, but it gets the job done," I had said to Harry as I completed the construction.

"That might be the ideal motto for your business card," Harry had responded with a grunt before returning to his friends in the back of the bar.

Although I had left my business card as it was, the phrase returned to my mind every time I crossed through that doorway into the Chicago Magic shop.

I'd be the first to admit the store is—in a word —*disorganized*. It's not like there's some subtle level of organization going on which isn't immediately visible to the eye. There isn't. It's just sort of a mess. Nathan had done a great job of creating at least a bit of order out of the chaos, but we still had a long way to go.

The section of the store devoted to gags and gag gifts reflected that organizational structure, but in miniature. Which meant it was impossible to find anything.

Consequently, it took me longer to locate what I was looking for than it really should have. But after several moments of shoving aside fake vomit and joy buzzers and snake-filled cans of mixed nuts, I found what I was looking for.

Moments later I set a small cardboard box on the table in front of Mark Kelly and Harry.

"This was a big seller, back in the day," I said as I folded back the top flap and pulled the device from the box. "There were several different versions manufactured, but I've always preferred this one."

"Yes, with this one the effect is cleaner," Harry agreed.

I placed the plastic box on the table. It was about nine inches tall and with a curved top reminiscent of a mailbox but painted in industrial gray tones. It certainly didn't look fancy. On the upper half of the front panel was a clear window, but it revealed only darkness within. The top of the device was adorned with a simple metal slot, with black rollers visible within. The words "Counterfeit Bill Detector" were stenciled in small letters across the front.

"What's it do?" Kelly said as he peered at it doubtfully. I could tell he was wondering how this plastic tchotchke was related to his pending phone call.

"We used them all the time in the shop when I was a kid," I explained. "When someone would want to buy something using a twenty-dollar bill."

"Or higher," Harry added.

"A rare occurrence, but yes. Since the advent of credit cards, we rarely see cash anymore these days. Have you got a twenty I can use?"

Kelly seemed surprised at the request, but a moment later he had pulled a bill from his wallet.

I took the twenty and pretended to examine it closely. "We'd say something about how there'd been a lot of counterfeit bills being passed in the area recently, and so we'd gotten this counterfeit bill detector. We'd explain that it was designed to identify fakes. And then we'd take their twenty and insert it in the top."

As I said this, I inserted Kelly's twenty into the slot on the top of the device. A small motor immediately kicked in and pulled the bill into the box.

Two things then happened simultaneously. First there was a slight shredding sound. At the same time, through the small window on the front, we could see the shredded pieces of the bill as they dropped down out of sight.

These elements—the motor pulling the bill into the device, the shredding sound effect, and the apparent torn pieces floating past the viewing window—all combined to create a very realistic effect. It really looked and sounded like his twenty-dollar bill had been neatly shredded by the device.

Mark Kelly chuckled. "I'm sure that panicked a few people."

"It always got a great reaction," Harry agreed. "One guy almost took a swing at me once. So, I quickly showed him how the trick was done."

That sounded like a cue to me. I spun the device around and popped open a small hatch on the back. The unharmed twenty-dollar bill lay safely within the compartment. I pulled it out and held it up for inspection.

"And you think something similar happened with the Hitler painting?" Kelly said as he took the small machine and examined it more closely. I handed him the bill and he ran it through a second time.

"I would not be surprised," Harry said. "And, given what it probably cost to modify a paper shredder to safely pull off that effect, I would also not be surprised if your gallery owner has squirrelled it away somewhere. It would be quite the creation and he doesn't strike me as the type to destroy a piece like that willy-nilly."

Kelly set the device back on the table. "Now I understand the need for the—what did you call it?"

"The secondary convincer," I said.

"It absolutely focused our attention on those ashes and away from the shredder," he said.

"As intended," Harry said.

Kelly glanced at his watch. "Well, I've got to make my phone call now. Thanks guys—you've just made a multi-national insurance conglomerate very happy."

"That's all we ever wanted in life," I said.

"Mission accomplished," Harry added.

Kelly pulled his phone from his pocket and began to dial as he headed toward the door. I slid the device back into its box and stood up as well.

"Eli, can you grab me a refill while you're up?" Harry asked as he held out his now-empty glass.

"Sure thing."

"And Eli?"

I spun around. "What?"

"This time can you make it a *real* ginger ale and not that watered-down diet nonsense?"

Even at his advanced age, I realized I was rarely going to be able to get anything past Harry Marks.

* * *

"ARE YOU PERFORMING OR PRACTICING?"

I looked up to see Mark Kelly standing in front of me. Until a few moments ago, I had thought I was the only one in the bar.

"With me, it's sometimes hard to tell the difference," I said. "What can I get you?"

He waved this away. "No time, on my way to a meeting," he said. "I just wanted to stop by and thank you and your uncle for your help on that painting thing."

"The Hitler painting?"

"That's the one," he said with a grin. "You both were absolutely right. I turned in my report. The company leaned on the police and—one search warrant later—they uncovered the modified shredder."

"Harry was right: the gallery owner couldn't bear to toss it out. It was a work of art."

Kelly shrugged. "Or else he's just lazy or stupid. Or both. But they found the shredder, they found the original painting, and he confessed to having staged the whole thing. Fraud charges are pending."

"Your client has to be happy about that."

"Who knows. He's in insurance. How happy can he ever hope to be?"

I laughed. "I'll let Harry know that you stopped by."

"One other thing," Kelly said as he gestured toward the wall behind me. "Is there any chance I can buy that off of you?"

I turned. He was pointing at the counterfeit bill detector, which I'd placed next to the cash register. I'd left it there after our earlier meeting. It was easier than going to the trouble of walking next door and finding a place for it on that messy gag gift shelf.

"As a memento?" I suggested.

"Something like that."

"Here, why don't you take it, on the house," I said as I grabbed the small machine and handed it to him across the bar. "As it turns out, people who use cash to buy drinks don't find this thing as funny as you might think."

"Go figure. Thanks!" He hefted the box in his hand as he headed toward the door.

With nothing else to do and no one to talk to, I did what I should have been doing for the past hour.

I picked up my deck of cards and began to practice.

As expected, it was slow going. Improvements, when they came, were at best incremental.

MAGICIAN IN TROUBLE

I t was clearly a mix-up.

    Not as bad as the time my agent sent me to a bachelorette party and sent Sexy Rex *(The Stripping Fireman)* to the Handleman Bat Mitzvah.

But it was clearly a mistake, nonetheless.

That was my first thought when I turned onto the street where my GPS had guided me. Ahead of me I saw the road filled with squad cars. I recognized logos from the Anoka County Sheriff's Department and the Minnesota State Highway Patrol, along with other unfamiliar vehicles with flashing lights. A deputy held up a hand to impede my progress and then approached my driver's window.

"Do you live on this block, sir?" he asked, his voice a studied monotone designed to both produce anxiety and maintain order.

"Um, no," I stammered. "I'm here for a gig, um, a show."

He raised an eyebrow at me. "You're not, by any chance, a magician, are you?"

This hardly seemed the time to deny it, although I had been

in situations in the past when that might have been the most prudent choice.

"Yes, officer. Yes. Yes I am."

He reached up to the radio on his shoulder and depressed a button.

"He's here," was all he said.

He then stepped back and waved me through. I put the car in gear and crept forward into the flashing circus at the center of the block.

* * *

THERE HAD BEEN nothing in the booking which had flagged it as unusual, except that it came in last-minute. But even that wasn't completely out of the ordinary. Performers often ran into scheduling issues—illness, family problems, travel snafus— and so a call from my agent wondering if I was available for a fill-in gig in a couple hours was not completely unheard of.

So, I'd packed my small bag for a walk-around set—with a few additional items in case a sit-down presentation arose— punched the address into the GPS and hit the road. I'd never been to the town of Nowthen, Minnesota, although I was pretty sure I had driven through it in the past. It was that kind of town: you drive through it and barely remember you'd been there.

Except for this visit.

Once I got through the barricade, I inched the car forward and was directed by another deputy into a space, haphazardly sandwiched between a fire truck and an ambulance. He gestured me out of the car and I followed, returning seconds later to grab my bag.

"This is the guy," the deputy said by way of introduction to a small cluster of very serious looking uniformed officers. The one who appeared to be in charge—a large, bald man who loomed over me—gave me the once over.

"I'm Sheriff Martin. You're here to see Leon Pearson?" he asked, his voice coming out like a gravelly growl.

The client's name was in my phone, but it didn't feel like the right time to start digging for that device. I racked my brain. "Yes, I think that's the name," I said.

"He's been asking for you."

"Me in particular?"

"You're the magician, right?"

I nodded. "Yes."

"Well, he said he'd come out peacefully after he sees the magician."

"Peacefully?" I repeated.

Sheriff Martin ignored this, putting a hand on my shoulder as he directed me toward a dark van several feet away. "Here's the situation: We think he's in there alone and we think he's armed. He threatened the mailman a couple of hours ago and vaguely suggested he was in possession of a weapon. That's what brought us out here."

"He threatened a mailman?" At the moment, I appeared to be programmed to only repeat words, not generate any original syllables of my own.

"Something about being tired of only getting bills and bad news," the older officer said. "We were able to get him on the phone, but he won't come out. Says he booked a magician and that's who he's waiting to see. That would be you."

We'd reached the rear of the van. Through the open doors I could see an array of gear and artillery. The older man looked up at a younger officer in the van.

"Get him a vest," Sheriff Martin said and then turned to me. "It seems he wants a magic show, so that's what we're going to give him," he said. "Do a couple tricks and then see if you can get him to come out."

Another man pushed his way toward us, grumbling as he

did. He was dressed in a suit, which made him stand out in the sea of uniforms.

"Martin, you're just handing him a hostage, is that it?" the man said in a loud whisper. It was so loud that it may have been louder than his normal voice. "That seems like a bad, bad idea."

I didn't know who this guy was, but I was liking the way he thought.

"Look, Swanson, I'm doing everything I can to deescalate this matter. He called for a magician; so, unless you know of a deputy who can pull a rabbit out of a hat, I say the smartest thing we can do right now is give Pearson what he wants."

The young officer in the van handed him a heavy flak vest, which the older officer quickly examined.

"Here," he said, pushing it in my direction. "Put this on."

I held the vest gingerly and then handed it back to him. "I can't wear that."

"What?"

"I can't wear that," I repeated.

"Good idea," Martin said as he took the vest. "No sense getting him riled up by taking an offensive posture."

I shook my head. "Actually, the vest will cover my pockets and inhibit my movements. If you want me to perform magic, it will have to be without the vest."

"This is insane," the man in the suit muttered.

"You got any better ideas?"

The two men faced each other down for several seconds. The man in the suit took a step back as he shook his head.

Sheriff Martin turned back to me. "Look, he seems like he's really on edge."

For a moment I wasn't sure who he was talking about. The man in the suit? The man in the house? To be honest, it pretty well described my current state of mind as well.

"Do what you can to calm him down," he continued. "Do a

couple tricks. Entertain him. Then see if you can coax him outside."

"If my tricks are bad enough, maybe that'll force him out. I've been known to clear a room," I joked. They stared back at me. "Got it. Do a couple tricks. Coax him outside."

I began to walk toward the house.

"And whatever you do—"

I turned back. The Sheriff and his team were staring at me. "Yes?"

"Whatever you do, just don't make things worse."

I couldn't help but smile. If I have one mantra as a performer, that was probably it.

* * *

I WAS ABOUT HALFWAY across the front lawn when my common sense caught up with me. Was this really the wisest course of action?

I looked at the house, which was a small rambler. It appeared identical to the houses on either side, paint color being the primary differentiator. The one in front of me appeared to be dark blue, with white trim. The shades were drawn and no lights were visible within, although the porch light was on. Unlike the houses on either side, the front door was painted red. I vaguely remembered this design touch indicated a welcoming environment.

I hoped that was going to be the case.

I stepped up to the door and looked for a bell. I couldn't find one, so I knocked. My first attempt was so soft I could barely hear it myself. I tried again, this time putting some force behind three sharp raps. It still sounded like a very weak woodpecker who'd lost the will to live.

However, it seemed to have registered. Leon Pearson must have been watching from inside, because the front door opened just a crack. I could see he had the security chain on. I could also see he looked like a wreck. Through the crack in the door, I could only see one eye (bloodshot) and a bit of his face (unshaven). His voice was a croaky whisper.

"Are you the magician?"

I nodded. "Yes, Mr. Pearson. I'm Eli Marks. The magician."

He stared back at me. "How do I know you're really the magician?"

The question stumped me. I had certainly witnessed several situations where performers had proved to me that they absolutely *weren't* magicians. But I was coming up short on an idea of how to prove I was. If I'd had a magic wand and a top hat with a rabbit in my hand, would that have persuaded him?

I stood there for several seconds and then an idea occurred to me. I fell back on the same words magicians have uttered since the dawn of ... well, since the dawn of magicians.

"Um, think of a card."

He stared back at me.

I continued, pretending he was the most helpful of audience volunteers. "Are you thinking of a card," I said as I slowly —oh so slowly—reached into my coat pocket.

He studied me closely. I sensed he was poised to slam the door.

I pulled a boxed deck of cards out of the pocket.

"Have you thought of a card?"

He nodded, doing it so gradually it appeared to be happening in slow motion.

"And what card did you think of?"

He continued to stare at me. Finally, I detected a weak whisper.

"Three of spades."

"Three of spades," I repeated way-too cheerfully. I slid the deck of cards out of its cardboard box. "Well, if I weren't a magician, could I make your card—the three of spades—reverse itself in this deck of cards? Like this?"

I made a vague magical gesture and then spread the cards so that he could see them. He looked down at the cards, then up at me to make sure I wasn't doing something tricky. Then back at the spread of cards in my hands.

It appeared to be a completely normal deck of cards. All the cards were different, but one card was face down in the deck.

I reached into the spread and pulled the card out, delicately flipping it over so he could see the face of the card.

It was the three of spades.

Through the crack in the door, I could see his one eye go wide. He closed the door for several seconds and I could hear him futzing with the security chain. A moment later, he swung the door open—not all the way open, but wide enough for me to step through.

As he closed the door behind me, oddly only one thought occupied my mind: Although it had gained me access to the house, I had just burned off a nice ten-minute routine. I hefted my bag, hoping I'd brought enough stuff to get me through this.

Whatever *this* turned out to be.

* * *

THE IMPRESSION I'd gotten from outside was correct: There were no lights on in the house. However, the spotlights the Sheriff's department had aimed on the exterior did a remarkably good job of providing plenty of illumination within.

The lights also added an eerie quality to the space, forcing long shadows on the wall, like a stark blue sunset was exploding just outside the front windows.

Leon waved me toward the living room, which was getting the most benefit from the spotlights outside. Furniture consisted of a worn couch, a side table, an easy chair, and a coffee table. The room was a little messy, but the key item or items I was looking for—a gun or guns—were not immediately visible.

I turned to my left and could see a small dining room beyond. The dinner table looked to hold the remains of a single meal, with the three other chairs set in an orderly fashion around the table. What looked like a large family photo was hanging on the far wall, but the long shadows from the spotlights made it hard to see any detail.

Here in the living room, a big TV sat on a stand positioned in one corner. *The Golden Girls* was playing silently. Betty White must have just said something stupid, because Bea Arthur was giving her a death-beam stare. Although the volume was off, somehow I felt like I could still hear the echo of canned laughter.

Once I had a sense of my environment, I turned to survey my host. He was somewhere in his forties and about three inches shorter than me; a bald spot on the top of his head was clearly in the process of spreading to the rest of his scalp. He wasn't shaking, exactly, but he was sort of vibrating. He was clearly nervous. He was wearing an out-of-style suitcoat, which hung on him poorly; he'd either lost weight or had never really grown into his father's suit.

He wasn't holding a gun, but the coat was bulky enough to hide a weapon and a couple good-sized cats as well. In fact, it might have been my imagination, but it looked like the left side of the coat was drooping down further than the right. Was there a bulky object in that left pocket? I really couldn't be sure one way or the other, so I decided the best course of action was to proceed as if there was.

The coffee table was cluttered with several empty beer bottles and two mostly empty bags of chips. Leon cleared them away quickly, disappearing from the room for a moment. Seconds later he was back; the trash was gone, and he'd grabbed a straight back chair from the dining room. He set it in front of the coffee table and gestured that the couch was mine.

"So, you'd like a magic show," I said as I settled in, really trying to sound upbeat and cheerful. I was probably overdoing it.

"I was supposed to have a magician before," he said quietly. He wasn't making eye contact. "When I was ten. For my birthday. It didn't happen. Like a lot of things didn't happen."

He was staring at the coffee table. We sat without speaking for several seconds. I was running some possible responses through my head, but before I could settle on one, he spoke again.

"It didn't happen," he repeated. "And, you know, I still want that magician. So, I called and booked a magician." He looked up at me. His eyes were really watery; he wasn't crying but was right on the edge of tears. "I'm sorta having a bad week."

I nodded. "Do you want to talk about it?"

I'm not sure he actually heard me, but he kept talking. "I lost my job, my wife left me, she took the kids, I don't have any money, I have nothing but debts. And I'm just having a bad week."

I am not proud of it, but my first thought was, well, looks like I'm not getting paid for this one. But I quickly shoved that selfish notion aside.

"Perhaps a little magic can brighten things up," I said, again turning the cheerful knob up higher than probably necessary. "Do you like card tricks?"

He stared back at me vacantly.

"I don't know. Is that what most people like?"

I'd been reaching for a deck of cards, but his query stopped me cold. I had to admit, no one had ever posed that question to me. I had a lot of card tricks in my repertoire, but I'd never really stopped to consider this existential question: Was that what most people liked? Or was it simply what I liked doing?

"Well, I've got card tricks, coin tricks, tricks with rope, with rubber bands, a cups and balls routine," I rattled off quickly, pushing that larger question out of my mind for the time being. Instead, I tried to think about the sort of tricks he might have seen at the ten-year-old birthday party that never happened. I'm sure balloons had been on the program, maybe a coloring book illusion, probably some form of hippity-hop rabbits. And sponge balls. Lots of sponge balls.

I had none of those. Just cards, coins, rope, rubber bands and cups and balls. And a couple paperbacks for a book test, if it came down to that. Which I hoped it wouldn't.

"Cards are okay," he finally said.

"Well, since you seem to like the Three of Spades, let's do a little something with that card." I quickly sorted through the deck in my hand and found the card. I handed it to Leon while I reached for the black sharpie in my pocket. He clutched the card but watched my hand very closely. He seemed relieved to see it was just a magic marker as I pulled it from my pocket.

"Leon, go ahead and sign your name across the face of the card, just so we can make sure I'm not doing anything tricky." I uncapped the pen and handed it to him.

He slowly and deliberately signed his name on the card, taking far longer to write four letters than I might have expected. Once he appeared satisfied with the result, he tentatively handed back the card.

I blew on it, to make sure the ink was dry, and then launched into my routine. Under normal conditions, I do this modified Ambitious Card routine pretty quickly, getting some laughs with how swiftly the card jumps to the top of the deck, along with all the variations I'd added. However, I got the immediate sense that doing *anything* quickly would increase Leon's anxiety. It seemed pretty clear that my primary goal, if I had one, was to make Leon less and not more anxious.

I buried the card in the deck and then gave it a tap. I looked at Leon. "So, your Three of Spades is somewhere in the middle of the deck, right?"

Leon nodded as he stared at the deck.

"But you're a fan of the Three of Spades and it's a fan of you, so just like that, your card has jumped to the top of the deck."

I snapped my fingers to indicate this action and Leon actually jumped at the sound. I proudly flipped the card over.

It was the Six of Diamonds.

"Oops, looks like I did something wrong, sorry," I began as I prepared to correct this apparent mistake. "Let's find your card again."

I flipped the deck over and scanned through the cards for the Three of Spades. Leon watched me closely, his eyes locked on the spread of cards.

"That's weird," I said, sticking closely to my usual patter. "It's nowhere in the deck. I seem to have lost your card."

Usually, this point in the trick gets a bit of reaction from the audience; an 'ooh' or an 'aah' as they realize their card has disappeared entirely from the deck.

Leon, as the situation had already made clear, was not my typical audience.

"You lost the card?" he said, sounding frantic. "You don't know where it is?"

I put out a hand to reassure him. "Don't worry. I know where it is."

"But you said you lost it and it isn't there. You screwed up."

I quickly reached into my pocket and pulled out the Three of Spades. "It's okay, Leon. It's right here. Right where I put it. It's just part of the act."

"Part of the act," he repeated, but I didn't get the sense he was fully understanding the situation.

"It's a common trope with magicians," I explained. "We call it Magician in Trouble. You pretend to make a mistake. But you really didn't. It's just part of the show."

"So, the magician's really not in trouble?"

I shook my head, trying to sound as sympathetic as I could. "Standard procedure. I always know where the card is."

"Why is that?

"Because I put it there."

He thought about this for a minute and while he did, I couldn't help flash back to the many conversations—okay, arguments—I'd had with my uncle Harry on the topic of Magician in Trouble.

"Excuse my French," Harry would say. "But in my opinion, Magician in Trouble is just a jerk move on the part of the performer. You've gone to all the trouble to win their sympathy and affection. You make an apparent mistake. The audience feels bad for you. And then you pull the rug out from under them and basically say, 'Ha! I tricked you. I was in charge all along.'" Harry shook his head. "A jerk move," he grumbled.

But I always disagreed with Harry on this point. "Harry, I don't think anyone in the audience ever really believes I'm in trouble. They know it's part of the act."

"What they *know* and how they *feel* are two entirely different matters," he'd mutter as he'd walk away, effectively ending the debate. For the moment, at least.

"Magician in trouble," Leon repeated slowly. He looked up at me. He was backlit by the lights from outside, but I could see the look of desperation in his eyes. "So, maybe I'm not really in trouble?"

No, Leon, I thought. You are definitely in trouble. But I figured that wasn't the answer he needed to hear.

"Sure, maybe you're not in trouble either," I said.

"Maybe I'm not," he repeated softly.

I made the executive decision that I'd successfully completed that trick. It was time to move away from Magician in Trouble to something that might have a more positive feel to it. I felt the deck of cards in my hand. As a performer, I'm not big on metaphors, but a thought occurred to me.

"It's really all how you look at it," I began, ad-libbing some new patter for a trick I'd been doing since I was a teenager. I'd learned it from my uncle Harry, who had learned it from the guy who had first devised it. I had done it hundreds of times and felt I was probably in a good position to improvise on it a bit.

"Cards are like life," I continued. I split the deck in two, flipping one half over in my hands. "Sometimes things get mixed up. Jumbled."

I quickly shuffled the two halves, combining the face up half with the face down half. I completed the shuffle, cut the deck, and then spread the cards for Leon.

"As you can see, the cards are pretty evenly mixed, some face up, some face down. A mess."

"A mess," Leon repeated softly. He ran his finger across the cards and then pulled his hand away, perhaps concerned he had crossed some imaginary line.

I smiled to reassure him, then squared the cards. I quickly cut to some random spots in the deck and flipped it over, reinforcing the idea that all the cards were indeed mixed, face up and face down.

"But you know what, Leon?" I said as I gave the cards another cut and another shuffle. "Even when things are completely jumbled up in our lives, you know who has the power to put things right?"

He stared back at me blankly. Once it became clear he wasn't going to answer, I continued as if that had been my plan all along.

"We do," I said. "We can put things back in the right order."

I began to snap my fingers and then thought better of it; the last time I'd done that, it had spooked my audience-of-one more than I liked. So, instead, I waved my hand over the tabled deck.

"And just like that, order is restored."

I spread the deck across the tabletop. All the cards were now facing the same direction. They were all face up.

Except for one card.

I gestured for Leon to flip it over. He reached across and tentatively nudged the card from the spread and turned it.

It was the Three of Spades.

Although he was still backlit, I could see Leon's face enough to recognize when he burst into a big smile. He laughed softly as he picked up the card and examined it.

For the first time, I really truly appreciated the name of that trick.

Triumph.

Triumph, indeed, I thought.

I didn't want to lose momentum but wasn't sure what I could do to help keep this positive vibe rolling.

And then I remembered a variation on the trick Uncle Harry had shown me, one that allowed the spectator to take charge of the action. The trick I had just done was perfected by Dai Vernon; if I was remembering properly, it was based on a gimmicked trick by Theodore DeLand. However, the variation I was trying to remember had been put together by Bob Hummer.

I shook my head, trying to escape this unnecessary cascade of attribution. I needed to focus on *how* the trick was performed, not a chain of evidence on who had created it.

As the steps of the routine began to come in focus in the back of my brain, I scooped up the cards and quickly counted out two piles of twenty.

"You know, Leon, it's not just magicians who can do this trick," I said as I tried to keep count of the cards as I was dealing them out. "Anyone can create a mess. And anyone can fix it."

"Really?" he said. He was still looking at his Three of Spades.

"Really," I said. I slid one packet of cards toward him. "Let's do the trick together."

Leon took the cards and then earnestly followed my every move, mirroring each step with his own small packet of cards.

"First, count out ten cards," I said. "And then flip that pile over, face up."

Leon moved slowly, working diligently on the assignment. Once he was done, he looked up expectantly.

"Okay, now let's create a mess," I said. I took a card from the face up packet and started a new pile, then took one from the face down group. I alternated the process, taking one card from each packet, so that every other card was face up in this new pile.

Leon closely followed each step as I made it, making identical moves with his packets.

I spread the cards in this new packet, revealing a neat mix of cards, face up and face down. Leon did the same with his packet, touching the cards to reassure himself that they really were a mess.

"The cards are certainly a mess, aren't they?"

Leon nodded.

I squared my packet and Leon did the same with his.

Then I stopped.

This was the point where the trick got, well, tricky. This portion of the routine was very procedure heavy; and not procedure just for the sake of making things complicated. I had to complete the proper steps in the exact right order. Or I'd end up making a bigger mess than I'd started with.

Which, under the circumstances, didn't strike me as a particularly good idea.

I'm pretty sure I sounded confident as I directed Leon in the next series of moves, but it was pure acting on my part. I was mentally scrambling, hoping the sequence I was following was correct, but never really absolutely certain of the directions I was giving.

Finally, we each had our packets face down in front of us. Leon looked up at me, his eyes wide in anticipation.

"So, we made a mess, didn't we?" I said, doing a sort of standard recap of the actions we'd just completed. Usually when I did this, it was to reinforce the idea of how much free choice the spectator had or the fairness of the procedure.

But right now, I was doing it just to buy some time. The more time it took before I revealed the end of the trick, the longer I had before things potentially went wrong.

"We had face up cards, we had face down cards," I continued. "Utter chaos, am I right?"

Leon nodded. "We made a mess," he agreed.

"And then we took some very specific steps, didn't we?" As I said it, I was hoping against hope that those steps had, in fact, been the correct steps.

"Yes, we took steps to fix our mess," Leon said. His voice was just above a whisper.

"Let's see how those steps we took helped our situation." I gestured toward his packet of cards as I slowly—oh-so slowly—began to spread my own packet.

Leon pushed awkwardly on his cards and they were gradually revealed. All the cards—all twenty—were face down. I glanced down at my own packet which, mercifully, was similarly correct in its orientation. I breathed a sigh of relief; I have no idea how audible it was, because whatever sound I made was covered by laughter.

Actual laughter. Coming from Leon.

He was smiling brightly, first at the cards, then at me. Then back at the cards.

"It was a mess," I could hear him muttering. "An utter mess. And then I took some steps. And the mess went away." He looked back at me. "The mess went away."

"That's right, Leon," I said. "You've always had the power to straighten up the mess." For a second I was worried I was sounding too much like Glinda in *The Wizard of Oz*, but Leon didn't seem to notice.

Leon was still smiling broadly. "I can straighten up the mess."

"Yes, you can."

I was about to gather up all the cards, but I suddenly realized the image in front of Leon—order out of chaos—was a good one to let linger, if only for a few minutes more.

"So, how did you like the magic show?" I said, once again sounding cheerier than necessary.

"I liked it a lot," he said. He was still smiling, his fingers grazing the spread of cards in front of him.

"So, what do you say we go outside and straighten up this other mess?" I suggested. I tensed as I asked the question, not sure if this sudden pivot might shift his mood in a less positive direction. He stared at me blankly for what felt like a long moment.

"Sure thing," he said as he suddenly stood up. "Let's go fix this thing."

I got up as well and grabbed my bag. I decided to leave the cards where they were; I didn't want to break the mood. And I could certainly afford to lose the cost of one deck of cards.

Leon began to move toward the front door, but before he got far, I tentatively reached out and touched his shoulder. He spun around. A flash of *something* shifted across his expression.

"What?"

Somehow, I maintained a cool, almost indifferent air. It certainly did not reflect what was going on inside me.

"You know, it's pretty warm outside tonight," I said casually.

I gestured toward his suit jacket. "You probably don't need that."

He considered this for a moment. "You're right. I probably don't."

He let the bulky jacket slip off his slim frame and drop to the ground. I heard a padded clunk as the jacket landed on the hardwood floor. It might have been his phone in one of the pockets. Or it might have been something else.

I opted not to dwell on it and headed toward the door, glancing back to make sure I had Leon in tow. He was following me, but he stopped to take one last look at the spread of cards on his side of the coffee table.

I opened the door and stepped out, immediately holding up a hand to indicate ... well, to indicate that I was okay enough to be able to hold up a hand. Leon followed me, and we both squinted at the bright lights which were nearly blinding us. I wrapped a protective arm around his boney shoulder and he leaned into me as we started up the front walk toward the street.

Things had been strangely quiet when we stepped out of the house, but that changed quickly. In an instant we were surrounded by uniforms and loud, barking voices. I hung onto Leon and squinted into the lights until I made out the figure of the large, bald guy in charge. We moved toward each other, each pushing through the throng of law enforcement which had descended on us.

"Sheriff Martin, this is Leon Pearson," I shouted over the din to the imposing man. "He's had a rough week and realizes he has to correct some mistakes."

"Yes, I do," Leon said, although his voice was so soft, I was probably the only one who heard him.

"Mr. Pearson, if you'll come with me, we'll see what we can do to help you out."

Sheriff Martin took Leon by the arm and looked to me to

release my grip on the small man. I hesitated a moment, but the Sheriff gave me a reassuring nod, so I let him go. Leon was immediately swept away by the throng, the crowd appearing to steer him toward an Anoka County Sheriff's vehicle.

I found myself suddenly alone in the front yard, with all the attention now focused on getting Leon quickly searched and into the vehicle. With my part in the drama now behind me, I turned toward where I had parked my car, not sure if I was blocked in by emergency vehicles or if I could make an easy exit.

There was considerable chatter all around me, so I'm surprised I heard a weak voice calling my name. I turned to see that it was Leon. They were just putting him in the backseat of a squad car, but he was resisting the action, trying to get my attention.

"Eli," he shouted again, his voice finally cutting through the commotion. Everyone seemed to quiet as I stopped.

"Yes, Leon," I shouted back.

"Be sure to mark this date in your calendar," he yelled back, his face breaking out in a wide grin. "I'll want to be sure to book you again for my birthday. Next year!"

With that he was maneuvered into the backseat and moments later, lights flashing and sirens blaring, the car made its way down the block and disappeared around the corner.

As I headed back to my car, a phrase often employed by my uncle Harry popped into my head: *"If you can book enough repeat business, Eli, you will never, ever need to advertise."*

I smiled wryly. If I continued to survive these engagements, I appeared to be on my way to that goal, one gig at a time.

THE DEATH OF THE BLACK KNIGHT

"Do you want to know the definition of an optimist?" Uncle Harry posed this question as he climbed into my car. And *climbed* was the right verb; I had noticed it was becoming more and more of a challenge for him to both get in and get out of my tiny Mini-Cooper. It got me thinking it might be time to upgrade to a more grown-up car, if only to make it easier to transport him.

"What's the definition of an optimist?" I knew I was just acting as his straight man, a role I'd been happy to play since about age fourteen.

"An optimist is a man in his eighties about to sign a thirty-year mortgage," he said with a chuckle.

Most of the morning's jokes and quips had been real estate-related, to reflect our current mission. Although we both knew he was clearly nowhere near the signing stage. When it came to buying a new home, Harry was—as he stated repeatedly as we ambled from Open House to Open House—"just looking, thank you very much."

He and Franny had been considering moving out of her

small house in Richfield for two key reasons. The first was stairs, of which the rambler had too many.

When Harry had lived above the magic store, Chicago Magic, he had a set of stairs to climb each day which would have given a mountain goat pause. The move to Franny's place offered stairs which weren't nearly as steep but were instead more plentiful: the steps to get down to the laundry room and the steps to get up to their master bedroom. With his knees and her back, they both knew it was time to start thinking about seeking new living arrangements.

So, the first consideration for moving was to find a place that consisted of just one level, eliminating stairs insofar as possible.

The second consideration was one of upkeep: Harry had no objection to paying someone to cut his grass, rake his leaves and shovel his walk. He just couldn't find a person or service who would complete the tasks with any level of consistency. Which drove him crazy.

"Service economy my eye," he would growl when he once again faced the problem of finding yet another company to handle these relatively small tasks. "I swear, it's easier to buy high-grade opium on the street than to find someone to shovel snow in this city."

These two considerations—stairs and landscaping—narrowed their options primarily to townhomes in small planned neighborhoods, mostly situated in the first ring suburbs around Minneapolis.

Our mission on this particular morning was one of elimination: Franny had given Harry a list of Open House properties to approve or veto. Once he'd cast his vote, the next stage would be for both of them to visit the potential properties together and narrow them down to one on which they could both agree.

The first three places had just been drive-bys, because that was all Harry required to jettison the houses from the master list. However, the fourth option seemed to hold some possibilities.

"Quiet neighborhood, that's good," he said as he scanned the circle of about twenty townhomes in the cul-de-sac. "All the houses aren't painted the same, that's a nice touch. Oh, and one even still has a few Halloween decorations up. That's a plus—in my mind, people are in too much of a rush to shed the trappings of my favorite holiday these days."

In addition to its Halloween embellishments, the townhome also sported an "Open House" sign, indicating it was our destination. I pulled up to the curb while Harry continued his initial appraisal.

"It appears to be all one level, no front steps, an attached garage," he quickly listed. "So far, there's no reason not to go in and find out why it won't work."

With that positive assessment, I turned off the car and hurried over to the passenger side to offer assistance to Harry. He waved it away, but I grabbed his elbow and helped him out of the low car anyway.

Harry surveyed the front of the house as he got his sea legs. "Well, my initial assessment is that I don't hate it."

"High praise, indeed," I said as we started up the short driveway toward the front door.

"Hey, wanna buy some Halloween decorations?" The voice came to us from a life-sized pirate skeleton. We turned to the sound just as a face appeared from behind the boney figure. The fellow was in his thirties and was in the midst of disassembling the figure, placing the pieces in one of several large plastic tubs. "They're priced to move."

"No thanks," I said. "I live in an apartment."

"Perhaps you could include them in the sale of the house," Harry suggested. "There are buyers out there for whom an offer like that might just be the tipping point."

The guy shook his head. "Not in this neighborhood. Decorations like these can get you killed."

With that ominous pronouncement, he returned to his work and we made our way toward the front door.

* * *

"You've got all new appliances in the kitchen, a new roof, new video doorbell and security system, and all new carpet in the master bedroom," the realtor said in a quick, practiced recitation. "Plus, if you're interested, the seller would be happy to include the patio furniture at no additional cost."

The realtor, who introduced herself as Sybil Tewkesbury, was doing her best to sound *super* interested in the property. However, she also kept checking her phone, so this particular Open House may not have been her top priority.

Harry peered out the window at the patio and its now-included furniture. "That's nice," he said noncommittally. I could tell he was using the same affect he'd put on when buying a car; polite, but just this side of bored. "How about all those Halloween decorations? Are they included as well?"

I didn't think Harry was actually interested in decorations. Like me, he was curious about the odd statement made by the guy on the front lawn. How could Halloween decorations get one killed?

The question was clearly not one Sybil Tewkesbury was thrilled about answering. "Well," she stammered. "I suppose we could explore that. The thing is...the thing is, there were some issues between the previous owner and the Association Board about those, um, those decorations. So, personally, I wouldn't recommend heading down that path again."

"What sort of issues?" Harry said. He might not be interested in buying the house, but he was definitely intrigued by this story.

"Well, there was a lot of back and forth about the appropriateness and quantity of the items," she began. "Which, unfortunately, ended quite tragically."

"Tragically?" Harry and I said, accidentally in unison.

"Yes, sadly the owner was shot while giving out Halloween candy," she said quietly. This sudden drop in volume was odd, as we appeared to be the only ones with her in the house. "The police believe the incident was a direct consequence of the decorations."

"The owner was murdered?" I said quickly. "Over Halloween decorations? How did that happen?"

"That's interesting," Harry said, waving my questions away. "But aren't you required to disclose such an event as part of the sales process?"

"Well, yes," Sybil said with a nod. "Which I've just done. But normally, who wants to touch on such gruesome tales at an Open House? I'd be inclined to make something like that an element in the inspection process, if and when it comes to that."

"Wait, back up," I said, still not fully understanding her description of the events. "He was killed over Halloween decorations?"

"Like I said," Sybil replied, again using her quiet voice, probably in the hopes I'd do the same. "The police are looking at all possibilities."

"It was one of the neighbors and I have a pretty good idea which one it was," came a voice from behind us. We turned to see the guy who had been disassembling the decorations out on the lawn. He was lugging a full tub, which he stacked next to two others near the front door. "If you want my opinion, it was Claude Harrison. He shot Dave in cold blood."

"Did I mention the new washer/dryer combo?" Sybil said, gesturing that we should follow her out of the front entryway. But Harry ignored her.

"You think a neighbor shot him? Over the decorations?"

"A couple of the neighbors hated Dave's Halloween decorations," the man continued. "It was his favorite holiday, ever since we were kids."

"This is Ray, the late owner's brother," Sybil said. She sounded defeated, clearly feeling she had lost her fruitless battle to change the subject.

"What form did the neighbors' objections take?" Harry took a step closer to Ray and I followed.

"They filed complaints with the Association Board," Ray said as he pulled off his work gloves. He sported a couple days' worth of beard and looked like he'd been awake for that time period as well. "Claude Harrison is the President of the Board and he brought it up to a vote at an emergency meeting. The Board has final say on all exterior enhancements."

"They also have a charitable wing, it does a lot of good in the community," Sybil added, but I could tell her heart was no longer in it. She returned her attention to her phone.

"But Dave was too smart for them," Ray said with a grin. "You see, they objected to the number of decorations and the amount of light they gave off. I mean, you can toss around words like 'garish' and 'gaudy,' but that's all subjective. So, they went after him with hard numbers.

"And he came right back at 'em," Ray continued. "Dave presented photos of Christmas displays from the previous years, in which neighbors had far more decorations on their homes than he did. And their displays were giving off a lot more light as well. He was able to prove that a precedent had been established. It made Claude Harrison furious, but there was nothing he could do. So, instead, Claude shot him."

"However, the police can't substantiate that, am I correct?" Harry offered.

Ray shook his head. "Even though there were a ton of people around, no one saw him do it. I think he used a silencer.

But I can't prove it." He looked over at the realtor. "I'm going to go grab some lunch. I'll be back later to finish dis-assembling everything."

He looked at the two of us as he headed out the front door.

"Anyway, if she didn't mention it, there's new carpet in the master bedroom, a new security system, and new appliances in the kitchen."

And then he was gone.

* * *

"I GET the sense Franny's unlikely to add this house to her list of possibilities," I said as Harry and I headed down the driveway toward the car. "What with the murder and all."

"You'd be surprised. Franny's far more open-minded than you might think," Harry said.

"Yes but come on: A homicide took place right there in the house."

"Actually," said a female voice, "it wasn't in the house. It was outside, by the front door."

We both turned to see a woman walking a small, black Scottish Terrier. The woman, who appeared to be in her fifties, was bundled up against the cold winds which had settled on the Cities after Halloween. The dog looked very stylish, wrapped in its own tartan coat.

"I was there when it happened," she continued. "There were a whole bunch of us. Dave was joking with one of the kids and they were grabbing candy and laughing. And all of a sudden, he yelled, 'Call 911! I've been shot! Call 911!'"

"And the Board President was there as well?" Harry asked.

"Sure, Claude was there, but like I told the police, I didn't see him do anything. But it was a big crowd, a lot of kids coming and going."

"Does this neighborhood normally get a lot of kids on

Halloween?" I was thinking of our own situation on Chicago Avenue, where we had seen fewer and fewer trick-or-treaters each year.

"It did once Dave moved in," the woman said. "He created the perfect Halloween storm, and I'm not talking about the blizzard in '91. No, lots of scary decorations—with strobe lights and fog and weird sound effects—*plus* he gave away full-size candy bars. No fun-size for him."

"Don't get me started on the myth of fun-size candy bars," Harry grumbled to no one in particular.

"Once word got out, kids would come from miles around. Which was one of the things Claude hated," the woman said. She stepped closer and lowered her voice. "Claude doesn't like outsiders coming into our cul-de-sac with their kids on Halloween. He said Dave's set-up attracted the wrong element."

"Was he right?" Harry asked.

She shrugged. "It's Halloween, it's fun, but Claude doesn't like fun. I think that was his biggest beef with Dave, because Dave really loved Halloween. Oh my, you should have seen what he came up with every year. He had a ton of costumes and was always adding to his huge supply of decorations."

"You knew Dave well?" Harry asked.

"As well as you know any neighbor," she said. "Maybe a little better. We'd chat, exchange gossip. He'd carp about his freeloading brother, I'd complain about my lazy husband. You know, standard stuff. And then to see him shot, right in front of me. It was horrible."

She winced at the memory. I was ready to let her get on with her walk, but Harry wasn't finished exploring this gory tale.

"Can you tell me exactly what happened?" he asked in his most soothing tone.

"Well, like I told the police," she began. "It was a busy night. Lots of kids running through the neighborhood—some I recognized, some I didn't. I was taking our two little ones out on the circuit, while my husband stayed home to hand out candy.

"When we got here," she gestured up toward the house, "Dave was sitting in a chair by the front door, kibitzing with the kids. The strobe lights were going, there was fog on the ground. And sound effects galore: moans and screams. Dave was in costume, of course, all dressed up as that knight from that Monty Python movie. The one with no legs and bloody stumps for arms."

"The Black Knight?" I offered.

"That's the one. It was really gross but kind of funny: the chest plate, the helmet, the bloody stumps, all covered in blood. And just like in the movie, he'd yell at the kids as they took candy from the bowl, his voice all tinny in the helmet. 'Hey ghost: Just take one, you little monster!' Or, 'Hey, Spiderman, are you afraid to fight me?' Stuff like that."

She took a deep breath. I could tell it wasn't an easy story to re-live.

"Anyway, there was a big group when my kids and I arrived. We're waiting our turn to go take candy from the bowl, and Dave was joking and kidding, making fun of their costumes."

"And Claude was there?"

She nodded. "Yes, even though he had tried to get the decorations removed, he's a father with kids. And Dave was giving away full-size candy bars. Do the math. So, he bit the bullet and let his kids visit that house. And then all of a sudden, Dave yelled, 'Call 911! I've been shot! Call 911!'"

"And people did?" Harry asked.

"It took a few seconds to realize he was serious, but then everybody was on their phones in a flash," the woman said. "And the firetrucks and the EMTs were here super quick. One of the EMTs raced ahead of the others and pulled off Dave's helmet, tried to free his arms from the costume. Then the firemen made us all back up so they could get in and help him."

She sniffled a bit, then continued. "The irony was, if he'd been wearing an actual metal chest plate, the bullet might not have done any damage. Unfortunately, his was made of cardboard. They said he died in the ambulance."

"What did Claude do during all this?" Harry seemed to be determined to pull every last detail from this poor woman.

"I didn't really notice him until Dave's brother came running out of the house. He must have heard the fire engines. They had to pull him away from Dave, so the EMTs could work on him. And then he saw Claude and started yelling at him, 'You killed my brother, you killed my brother!' The police had to separate them, it got so ugly."

"But no charges were filed?" Harry asked.

She shook her head. "Not yet. There were plenty of witnesses, but no one saw anything. They couldn't find a gun. So, it's still a mystery."

She looked over at the few remaining decorations which Dave's brother still needed to pack away.

"End of an era," she said sadly. "Halloween's not going to be the same without Dave."

* * *

I WAS REMINDED of her story two days later as I carried a tray of drinks to some patrons in the back of the bar

I hadn't gone all out with the Halloween decorations this year, but the meager ones I'd hung up had started to sag and were clearly ready to be taken down. I dreaded the task, if only because clearing away the artificial cobwebs I'd placed in the corners would also probably involve cleaning out the real cobwebs right behind them.

But seeing the decorations reminded me of the death of the Black Knight.

I set the beers on the table where two of The Four

Horseman of Criminal Apprehension were sitting. Uncle Harry had given the foursome that nickname because all were involved in some form of criminal detection. They had, for some reason, picked my bar as their new hangout. It may have been because one of them was married to my ex-wife, but that had never been confirmed.

The cop in question, Homicide Detective Fred Hutton, grabbed one of the beers and gave the other a gentle push, sliding it in front of his tablemate, Carol Hollinger. Although she looked for all the world to be a stereotypical librarian, Carol actually ran the Minneapolis Police Department's forensics lab with an iron fist and an acerbic tongue.

At the next table sat my uncle Harry and two of his cronies from the Minneapolis Mystics: Mentalist Abe Ackerman and Ventriloquist Gene Westlake. It appeared that Gene must have gone to the Men's room; his seat was empty, but his coat was still hanging across the back of his chair.

Once I had their drinks in front of them, I turned back to the law enforcement professionals at the nearby table.

"Did you two hear anything about that murder in Bloomington? Where the fellow was shot while giving out candy on Halloween?"

"We got a call from the County on that one, because they were shorthanded," Homicide Detective Fred Hutton explained in his slow, lulling monotone. "Not much for us to do, though; victim died of a gunshot wound to the chest. No weapon has been found."

"The circumstances were pretty odd, though, don't you think?" I offered. "I mean, he's sitting right by his front door and someone shoots him while a crowd of parents and kids stand around watching?"

"With the distractions provided by the strobe lights and the fog and the sound effects, no one saw or heard anything," Carol Hollinger added. "At least, nothing helpful."

"So, questioning that neighbor he'd been feuding with didn't produce any results?" Harry asked.

Homicide Detective Fred Hutton was about to respond, but he was interrupted by Gene Westlake, who pushed past me to get to his chair.

"Well, that's annoying," Gene said loudly. "Just flat out annoying."

"What happened, Gene?" Abe Ackerman asked.

Gene Westlake was usually very soft-spoken, so this demonstration of emotion was highly uncharacteristic.

"Oh, I just got off the phone with my agent. Turns out, I lost another gig to that good-for-nothing Larry Bennett," he huffed. He took a quick sip of his drink of choice, a Diet Coke (no ice). "I don't need the work, of course, but it just irks me that phony is still getting paid for his malarkey."

Just about every magician and variety performer has a nemesis in the business: someone who gets more gigs and does it with less talent. For me, Simon Hartwell is the bane of my existence. For Gene Westlake, it was Larry Bennett.

"I wouldn't mind if it was someone *good*," he continued. "But that faker has been getting away with his nonsense for far too long. He just makes the rest of us look bad."

"What exactly is his 'nonsense,'" Carol asked.

"He steals like crazy," Gene said. "It's like that old saying: *'His act is good and original. The problem is, the parts that are good aren't original, and the parts that are original aren't good.'* That's Larry Bennett to a tee. Plus, the snake pre-recorded his finale," Gene sputtered. "Fake, fake, fake."

I'd never seen him this angry before. I exchanged a look with Harry.

"It's not uncommon," Harry explained, "for ventriloquists to close out their act with a song. A duet with their puppet. Jay Marshall and Lefty used to sing *'If I Had My Way.'* Jay Johnson and Darwin sang 'Send in the Clowns,' if I'm remembering correctly."

"Jimmy Nelson sang 'Rag Mop' and 'Hold That Tiger' as a medley. Just fantastic," Abe Ackerman added.

"Gene, you and Kenny did 'It Had to Be You' for years, and then you switched it out, right?" Harry said.

Gene was in the middle of taking a sip. He nodded. "Yes, I changed it to 'You're the Top.' It has a good back and forth and it's easier for me to customize the lyrics for corporate gigs. You know, 'You're the top, you're the best at retail. You're the top, you're the best at ad sales.' Clients eat that kind of stuff up."

"If you haven't seen Gene singing with his puppet, Kenny, you're missing something pretty spectacular," I said to Carol. "He can actually harmonize with the puppet."

"He studied with a Tuvan throat singer, of all things," Abe Ackerman said. "It's stunning."

Gene nodded modestly. "I don't know why I bothered to go to all that effort. I could just do it the way Larry Bennett does it —with a recording, for heaven's sake."

"How do you mean a recording?" Carol asked. I think Gene's emotional level had intrigued her.

"We all use pre-recorded music," Gene explained. "Your sound guy hits the *Play* button when you give him the cue, and you've got a nice background track to sing against. It's standard operating procedure. But this Larry Bennett clown, he went one step further: He pre-recorded his *puppet's* part of the song. So, it sounds like he's doing both voices, literally at the same time. In harmony no less. But it's really just a cheat."

"And clients don't mind that he's deceitful?" Carol asked.

"The poor saps don't have a clue, and if they did, they probably wouldn't care," Gene said with a sad shake of his head. "They don't give a hoot where the sound is coming from. They just want a good, clean show that finishes on time and doesn't bring down a torrent of emails from the trolls in HR."

Gene continued to rant about Larry Bennet and the damage he was doing to the art and craft of ventriloquism. But I'd stopped hearing him. Something he'd said reminded me of the death of The Black Knight. I glanced over at Harry, who also wasn't paying attention to Gene.

"So, let me ask you this," Harry said when Gene stopped talking long enough to take a quick breath. "That Halloween killing in Bloomington. Did you talk to the victim's brother at all?"

Homicide Detective Fred Hutton nodded. "We questioned him at length. He was inside the house during the evening, playing a video game of some sort. He did go out a couple of times to refill the candy bowl; apparently, the victim's costume rendered his limbs useless for the duration. But other than that, the brother didn't realize anything had occurred until he saw the flashing lights of the firetruck with the EMTs."

I remembered the woman walking the dog had casually referred to him as 'Dave's freeloader brother.' I wondered if there was more to it than that.

"Did you get a sense of any tension between the two brothers? Bad blood or anything?"

Homicide Detective Fred Hutton narrowed his eyes at me. "Not from the brother, no. In fact, according to him, he had made plans to move into his own housing within the next few weeks. He said his residence there was always intended to be temporary. But several of the neighbors did report loud arguments. However, by all accounts, the brother was in the house when the fatal, silent shot was fired."

"Was the property left to him in the will?"

"There was no will, but as the only surviving next of kin, the house—and all of his brother's assets—are his, once it clears probate."

I looked over at Harry. "Are you thinking about *Morrit's Donkey Disappearance* illusion?"

He nodded. "Yes, but coupled with something akin to the audio ploy used by our friend, Larry Bennett."

Carol Hollinger leaned forward. "What are you talking about?"

"It's obvious to us," Harry said as he sat back confidently in his chair. "The Black Knight was killed by his brother."

* * *

"WELL, the Karmic wheel has spun, my friends, and it landed with a thud on Larry Bennett."

It was about a week later and Gene Westlake was nearly skipping as he approached the Mystics table in the back of the bar.

"How do you mean?" Harry asked.

"I heard from my agent about that gig I lost to Bennett," Gene said as he slid into an empty chair. "Turns out, his finale crashed and burned. The client threatened not to pay him. They certainly won't be hiring him again. And I'm sure word of the fiasco has spread throughout the meetings and events industry."

"What went wrong?"

Gene continued to grin. "Apparently, the Luddite was still using CDs for his audio cues, for goodness' sake. When they hit the cue for the finale, something went wrong about thirty seconds into the song. The CD started to skip!"

"How soon did the sound guy figure out there was a problem and fix it?" Having had my own tech nightmares while on stage, I was curious as to how long Larry Bennett had been hung out to dry.

"Not soon enough, that's for sure," Gene said. "For some insane reason, he'd picked the song *'Don't Go Breaking My Heart'* as his finale."

"Like you said, the parts of his act that are original aren't good," Harry said with a laugh.

"And to add insult to injury, the CD skipped on the word 'heart,'" Gene continued. "Except it sounded like, pardon my French, the word 'fart.' And it repeated. Over and over and over again."

"For how long?"

"Long enough," Gene said. He was having trouble talking, he was laughing so hard. Harry and I couldn't help but join in.

"Well, this is a jolly group. What's so funny?"

I looked up to see Homicide Detective Fred Hutton was looming over us.

"We're just rhapsodizing about performance hijinks gone wrong," I said as I stood. "You want your regular?"

He shook his head and gestured for me to stay seated. "I'm on duty. I just wanted to stop by and let you two know you were right about the Halloween killing."

"So, it <u>was</u> the brother," Harry said, a tinge of pride in his voice.

"In fact, you were right on virtually every count," Homicide Detective Fred Hutton said as he pulled up a chair. There were plenty of seats available at our table, but for some reason he chose to grab one from his regular table. I imagine it was his way of keeping a separation between church and state.

"Let us guess what we got right," Harry said as he smiled at me. "First off, he killed his brother for money. That's the most common reason, after passion."

"Bingo," the detective said. "The house and the estate totaled over a million dollars. Our killer was dead broke, and his brother was tired of covering his gambling debts."

"He knew the fracas over the decorations had created a likely suspect in the Board President," I added. "And once he found out his brother was going to dress up as The Black Knight, he knew Halloween was the best time to do the deed."

"Exactly."

"And The Black Knight was the perfect costume," I continued. "Basically, he helped his brother into the outfit, then drugged him to knock him out. With the helmet over his head, no one could see he'd been slipped a mickey."

"And, since the character has no arms or legs, it made sense for him to be sitting there all night, stock still," Harry added. "Just this torso, yelling insults at the kids through his mask."

"But I thought he was drugged?" Gene Westlake said. "How could he yell at the kids?"

"He was out like a light," I said. "But the house was equipped with one of those video doorbells."

"Just like you throw your voice with your puppet, so too did the brother throw his voice, via the speaker on the video doorbell," Harry explained. "Everyone assumed it was the voice of our victim."

"It sounded a bit tinny, but that was fine, because it was supposedly coming from within the helmet, which was only a couple feet away," I added.

"And because the doorbell includes a video camera, the brother was able to see all the trick or treaters from inside the house," Harry said. "That allowed him to make specific comments about their costumes, which added verisimilitude to the effect."

"So far, you're batting a thousand," Homicide Detective Fred Hutton said. He wasn't actually smiling, but he did seem to be enjoying our recap of the fatal event.

"So, once the brother sees—via the doorbell cam—that the Board President, Claude Harrison is in attendance, he knows it's time to complete his plan," I said. "He shouts, 'I've been shot, call 911' into the doorbell speaker. And people in the crowd grab their cell phones and start dialing."

"Now, at this point I'm just guessing, but the woman we talked to told us Dave had a large supply of Halloween costumes," Harry said slowly. "I suspect one of those costumes might have been that of a fireman-slash-EMT."

He looked to Homicide Detective Fred Hutton, who merely nodded.

"And, just like the assistant dressed in the clown costume in *Morrit's Donkey Disappearance* illusion, the brother knew the EMT costume would cover a key moment in the crime," Harry continued.

"As the firetruck pulls up, the brother appeared—probably running around from the back of the house," I said. "He dove into the crowd, pushing them aside to get to the alleged victim. Under the cover of removing Dave's helmet, he took that moment to shoot his brother, fatally, at close range. With a silencer."

"Then, as the real EMTs ran up the driveway, he stepped away and blended into the confusion, before sneaking into the house again, via the back door," Harry said. "He quickly shed the costume and appeared, moments later, at the front door, confused and outraged."

Homicide Detective Fred Hutton continued to nod silently.

"I would guess, unless he was smarter than the average criminal, the costume is still among Dave's effects," Harry continued. "And that powder burns will be detected on the gloves."

"Right on all counts," Homicide Detective Fred Hutton said. "Plus, even though he deleted the videos recorded by the doorbell, he was unaware the security company stores all videos —deleted or not—for thirty days. In a very real sense, the stupid sap recorded all the evidence we'll need to convict him."

"Very thoughtful of him," I offered.

"Anyway," Homicide Detective Fred Hutton said as he stood up. "I just wanted to stop by and thank you for the tip. It made all the difference."

Without waiting for a response, he turned and headed toward the door.

I looked over at Harry. "Did he just give us a compliment?"

"I believe so, although he's likely to deny it," Harry said with a laugh. "And, like Halley's Comet, don't expect to see that event again for another eighty-some years."

I stood up as well, recognizing actual customers had wandered into the bar and would likely appreciate service. But then a thought occurred to me.

"Oh, should I block out Saturday for more Open House drive-bys?"

Harry shook his head. "I believe Franny and I have solved our housing issues and that we'll be staying put."

"But what about all the stairs?"

"We need to replace the washer/dryer, so we're just getting a smaller stacking unit, which will fit nicely into the mud room. So, no more traipsing down to the cellar to do laundry."

"But what about the stairs up to the master bedroom?"

"Franny had a brainstorm: On the main floor, we're knocking down the wall between the guest bedroom and the never-used office and turning that into the Master bedroom," he said. "The one upstairs then becomes the guest room."

"Slick," I said. "But what about your outdoor needs: shoveling, raking, cutting the grass?"

Harry smiled. "Remember when you were a teen and were always looking for ways to earn some pocket money? How you lamented that we lived above the store, so you couldn't hit me up to cut the grass and rake the leaves?"

I nodded. "That was one of the key reasons I started doing magic for kids' birthday parties—it was my only source of income. So, have you found a neighborhood kid?"

"Well, he lives nearby and although he's no longer a youngster, he still possesses an undeniable boyish charm."

It took a long moment, and then I got it.

"You're hiring <u>me</u>? I'm doing the lawn and the shoveling?"

"Not to worry, it will be at current rates. Plus, it will give me a chance to see you more often."

"I see you every day," I protested. "Every single blessed day."

"Aren't we a lucky pair?" Harry said with a grin as he held up his empty glass. "Now, be a dear and grab me a refill."

THE 38 STEPS

Has there ever been a four-a.m. phone call that was good news?

Possibly.

Like being awakened from a sound sleep to be told you've won the Nobel Peace Prize. But, even then, I'm sure there are plenty of Nobel laureates who would have happily waited until a more reasonable hour to receive such delightful information.

From the moment I was rudely awakened, I had no reason to think this call was from the Nobel Committee or that it would be delightful. And the ring tone supported that belief.

It was from my ex-wife.

After I'd gotten re-married, I had switched her tone from a song snippet (the Rolling Stones' *It's All Over Now*), to a more discrete yet still distinctive ring. The Settings on my iPhone informed me the tone I selected was technically called Old Phone. Whoever was in charge of naming ring tones had nailed it on that one: It sounded exactly the way phones did when Deirdre and I had first met. So, it seemed a fitting choice for her blessedly infrequent calls.

"Sorry to bother you so early," she said after I finished

fumbling and finally answered. Yet her manner didn't suggest she was in the least bit apologetic. That would have been out of character for Deirdre. She is no-nonsense times ten. "Fred needs to talk to you."

The Fred she was referring to is her newish husband, Homicide Detective Fred Hutton. She had hyphenated when they'd gotten hitched, giving her a moniker that always made me smile: Assistant District Attorney Deirdre Sutton-Hutton.

Sometimes, the universe has a sense of humor.

"Then why didn't Homicide Detective Fred Hutton place this call?" My voice came out thicker than anticipated. I think I was clinically still asleep.

"He thought it was too early."

"He was right. And yet you clearly felt no such compunction?"

"Not in the least."

"And why did your husband feel this need—albeit via surrogate— to call me?"

"There's a body in the morgue that came in overnight, a John Doe," she said. "Fred took a look through the guy's pockets. We think he may be a friend of yours."

"How do you figure?"

"It will make more sense once you're here."

"Sure thing. How does noon sound?"

"I'll see you in thirty minutes."

Before I could generate the beginnings of an argument, she had already hung up. I set the phone down as I struggled to sit up.

"What was that?" Megan's voice came from deep within her pillow.

"I have to go to the morgue. Do we need anything?"

"At the morgue? What do you mean?"

"You're dreaming. Go back to sleep."

I didn't have to suggest this twice. Before I'd even found my pants, she was already snoring quietly.

* * *

ALTHOUGH THERE HAD BEEN talk for years about moving the crowded Hennepin County Morgue from downtown Minneapolis out to the suburbs, that relocation had yet to occur. The drive was simple and straightforward: There was no traffic to speak of at this hour and parking was plentiful.

I had to ring a bell to gain entrance to the old two-story building. Once I was buzzed in, I nearly ran right into Deirdre.

"You made good time."

"It helps if ninety-nine percent of all drivers are home and asleep. What did you want me to see?"

By way of response, Deirdre turned and headed down a dimly lit corridor. Her heels made a clacking sound that echoed annoyingly through the building, although I imagine most of the occupants didn't really care one way or the other at this point. I scurried to catch up.

"Around midnight, someone discovered a body on the bike path which runs around Lake Harriet. The victim appeared to have fallen down the stairs. The ones that lead down from Penn Avenue."

"I know those stairs. They're like the stairs from *The Exorcist*, only scarier. They're really steep. And deadly."

"Well, they certainly were last night."

She made a sharp right, into a large and under-illuminated office. Through glass windows in the back of the room I could see a brightly lit exam room. Homicide Detective Fred Hutton was in conversation with a stern-looking woman in a white lab coat.

"So, is this considered a homicide?"

Deirdre shrugged. "Right now, it's in that fuzzy gray area.

For the time being, we're calling it a suspicious death. It would help if we knew who he was."

"And you think I knew him?"

"The District Attorney's office has its suspicions," came a booming if dull voice. Homicide Detective Fred Hutton had stepped into the room. He was holding a plastic evidence bag. "We in Homicide aren't yet quite as persuaded."

"The only thing they found on the guy was a small silk coin purse," Deirdre said as she gestured at the item in the bag her husband was holding. After a nod from her, he pulled it out and placed it in the palm of his gloved hand.

"I'm not familiar with that coin purse," I began, but Deirdre held up a silencing hand.

The detective snapped the purse open and pulled out a single coin. Even from a few feet away, it was pretty clear what it was.

"And I certainly don't recognize that quarter," I said. Forty minutes ago, I had been sound asleep and now I was here and didn't know why. Irritated didn't begin to cover what I was feeling.

"Turn it over," Deirdre instructed. Her husband did as he was told.

I leaned in closer. "It's a quarter with writing on it."

"Those are your initials," Deirdre said. "E and M, in black magic marker."

"Okay, I'll give you that. But surely there are other people with the initials E.M.," I said. "E.M. Forster comes immediately to mind. Edvard Munch. Ethel Merman. E.G. Marshall, when he was in a rush. Ed Marlo."

"Who's Ed Marlo?"

"A friend of my Uncle Harry's from Chicago," I explained. "A terrific magician. Actually, he called himself a *cardician*, because he mainly worked with playing cards. You know that one move I do, the snap change? He developed that along with—"

"It's your initials," she said sharply, cutting me off. "I recognized them. I certainly saw them enough on legal documents."

I looked down at the coin again. The letters did have a familiar aura to them.

"From the mortgage on our house, right? We must have initialed those things fifty times."

"I was thinking more of the divorce papers," she said. "It's a more indelible memory. But, regardless, those are your initials. And I know you do at least one trick which requires someone to put their initials on a quarter. I certainly saw it enough."

"Well then, perhaps you might recall that in that trick, I get the spectator to put their initials on the coin," I said, feeling myself slipping right back into our standard argument format. I resisted the urge to dive in headfirst. "It would hardly be all that magical if I make it disappear and re-appear with my own initials on it. Following that logic, I might as well go ahead and sign my own name on all my playing cards."

"I understand that," Deirdre snapped. She took a cleansing breath and continued. "There must have been a point when *someone else* did the trick for you and you signed the quarter."

"I have no memory of anyone ever doing a trick for me that involved a signed quarter."

"Well, maybe not. But it certainly must have been memorable for this guy." This came from Homicide Detective Fred Hutton, who had been watching us impassively. "The victim kept it in a very expensive coin purse. And he had it on him when he died. In fact, it was the only thing he was carrying. That traditionally suggests there was a strong, sentimental value attached to the object."

"Eli, they've run fingerprints and facial recognition on this guy and they're coming up with nothing," Deirdre said. She wasn't pleading with me, but she was getting as close to it as she was ever likely to get. "Can you recall any instance when you signed a quarter with your initials for someone?"

I was about to say no, but then I was hit with a sudden memory.

There had been one instance.

I was doing a trick with a sugar packet—*Very Sweet*, by David Gabbay —and I asked my spectator for a quarter. He said that not only did he not carry money, but he also made a point of never, ever signing his name to anything.

I don't know why I hadn't thought of it earlier. He was more than just memorable. He was absolutely terrifying. And he was also the best audience for magic I'd ever had.

"I know who it is," I said.

* * *

"MR. LIME," Deirdre repeated. "But I thought he didn't exist."

I looked down at the corpse on the table in front of me. "Well, he doesn't exist anymore. But this is definitely him."

He was covered by a sheet, with only his head visible. But I recognized him instantly. Pale, nearly translucent skin, pulled tightly around his skull. Gray hair specked with gray, if that was even possible. His mouth was closed (and mercifully, so were his eyes), but if his thin lips had been peeled back, I'm sure his teeth would be just as yellow as the last time I'd seen him.

When was the last time I'd seen him?

I certainly remembered the first time: I had been tricked into thinking I was heading into a gig at a mansion on Lake of the Isles, only to find myself performing for a creepy old man in a dark and mammoth living room. A handful of other encounters followed, each more terrifying than the last. It wasn't that he ever threatened me personally; it was instead the persistent feeling that things would be very negative for anyone who happened to find themselves on his bad side.

"Why did you call him Mr. Lime, again?" Deirdre said.

"It was the name he gave himself," I explained. "He liked old movies. He didn't want to give me his real name. He was a fan of *The Third Man* and I think thought of himself like the Orson Welles character in the film: Harry Lime. A charming, immoral monster."

"So, you don't know his real name?" Homicide Detective Fred Hutton was leaning on a nearby counter.

I shook my head. "No, and I don't know where he really lived. Or what his business really was. Not for sure."

"But you think he was involved in criminal activity?" Deirdre asked.

"It sure seemed like it," I said. "I know he hired Dylan Lasalle at one point to act as a drug mule."

"We never found any proof of that," Homicide Detective Fred Hutton said.

"As you told me at the time. Repeatedly," I said. "And although he knew all about the death of that film projectionist, I don't think he was personally involved. In fact, I got the sense that he wasn't personally involved in anything. Like he was a puppeteer, managing events but never getting his hands dirty."

"They got plenty dirty tonight," Deirdre said dryly.

I looked down at the delicate corpse on the table in front of me. Mr. Lime had always seemed—simultaneously—both tiny and immensely imposing. Not a bad trick, if you can pull it off.

"Was he dead before he went down the stairs?"

Deirdre shrugged. "It's unclear. But he was absolutely dead by the time he hit the bottom," she said.

"I wish I could help you," I said. "But I have literally told you everything I know about the guy.

I pulled the sheet back up over his head, but it didn't really work.

Even completely covered, I couldn't stop seeing that terrifying face.

* * *

THE SUN WAS JUST COMING up as I headed home.

The day was threatening to snow, but like it had the last few days, it felt like another empty threat. Megan had been disappointed we'd had no snow for our recent Thanksgiving dinner, but Harry had been quick to put a positive spin on it.

"The trouble with snow on Thanksgiving," he'd said. "Is that by the time mid-January hits, it feels like we've had snow *forever*. It makes for a long, cruel winter. Count your blessings and pass the potatoes."

I had opted to take the scenic route home from the morgue, circling around the chain of lakes which dominate the landscape in South Minneapolis. This circuitous path eventually led me around Lake Harriet, which inevitably took me to Penn Avenue. Without even really thinking about it, I pulled the car over and shut off the engine.

From my position behind the wheel, I could just see the top of the stairs which cut down the steep hill to the lake below.

I sat there for a while, not really sure why I had taken this longer route home. And then, still not sure why, I got out of the car and crossed the street. I stood for several seconds at the top of the precipitous concrete staircase.

The comparison with the famous steps from *"The Exorcist"* was a good one, but with one key difference: The steps in Georgetown at least have the civility to include a couple of lights. By contrast, the stairs leading from Penn Avenue down to Lake Harriet offered no such helpful illumination. Even with the sunrise nearly complete, the long, hard stairway was dimly lit and shadowy.

The fact that no crime scene tape obstructed the top or the bottom of the steps drove home the idea the Minneapolis Police Homicide Division wasn't convinced a wrongdoing of any kind had occurred here. Yet I couldn't imagine a reasonable scenario for a frail and wobbly old man to decide that midnight would be an ideal time for a quick jog around the lake. And that this treacherous stairway was the most efficient way to get there.

I started down the steps, taking generous advantage of its cold handrail to ensure my otherwise precarious balance. After ten steps, I began to wonder why more people hadn't tumbled down this particular stairway. The narrowness of the steps and their uneven spacing, certainly made falling the most likely outcome.

As I reached the twentieth step, I realized I was counting and wasn't sure why. But I kept at it, carefully navigating the incline until I reached the safety of the bottom. Although safety was a relative term: the steps emptied out onto a bike path and offered limited visibility prior to that final step. Luckily, no bicyclists were currently on the pathway, which gave me a moment to turn and look back up the steep slope.

Thirty-eight steps.

That was the number of concrete stairs Mr. Lime had tumbled down—*did he fall or was he pushed?*—just a few hours before.

Thirty-eight steps. Why did that phrase stick in my head? My brain was suggesting it was familiar without giving me any further clues as to why.

And then I figured it out. And I felt strangely sad for Mr. Lime. This might have been the first time I ever had.

As a fanatical film fan, he would have likely been intimately acquainted with Alfred Hitchcock's early film, *"The 39 Steps."* Even knowing him as little as I did, I suspected it might actually have been a favorite of his.

Would he have enjoyed the irony of missing that goal by merely one step? Had he been able to count the stairs on his way down, silently wishing for one more small bit of concrete before landing with a fatal thud at the bottom?

Or was he already dead before he began his journey down these lethal stairs?

I looked up the long flight. There was bright sun visible at the top, but precious little illumination for the majority of the stairway. If I was thinking this might be a visual metaphor for the answers I would be discovering in the days and weeks ahead—a light at the end of a shadowy tunnel—I was sadly mistaken.

There would be no light at the end of this mystery. At that moment, I knew just about all I would ever know about the odd death of an even odder man.

* * *

THAT DIDN'T MEAN I didn't think about it. I certainly did.

I had plenty of other thoughts to occupy my mind over the next couple of weeks, but the death of Mr. Lime on those thirty-eight steps was a frequent visitor. I was never able to reach any sort of satisfying conclusion, though. Just a series of random images from our limited encounters, mixed with the memory of his body in the morgue. And his final journey down those deadly steps.

"Are you still pondering that staircase death?" Uncle Harry asked. "Because you certainly aren't in the here and now."

Currently the *here* and the *now* consisted of the back room of Chicago Magic, the shop Harry had founded and which I was attempting to keep on life support. He'd agreed to spend an afternoon with me, sorting through the mountains of stuff which had accumulated over the years in the storage area behind the store.

"There's plenty of treasure back there," he had said on more than one occasion. Over the next few hours, I hoped to determine the veracity of that statement. I also wanted to clear out all the junk, which my gut told me made up the majority of the alleged prized inventory.

"I don't know why his death sticks with me so much," I said. "It's a puzzle I just can't solve."

"Are you becoming like our friend Mr. Strickland?"

"Yikes. I certainly hope not. I wouldn't wish that fate on anyone."

Mr. Strickland was something of a legendary customer in the magic shop. He wasn't, as far as we could tell, a practicing magician—not an amateur nor a professional. To the best of my knowledge, he did not belong to either of the rival magic clubs in town.

In all the years he'd been coming into the store, I don't believe I'd ever seen him perform even one trick. Yet he bought tons of magic from us.

Strickland appeared to have a singular goal: To find out how a trick was done.

Period.

That was the end of his interest in the illusion, regardless of how much he'd spent to get that information. He demonstrated zero interest in performing it. He was, in all recorded cases, merely after the secret.

Uncle Harry—who has hard and fast rules about selling magic before a magician is ready to perform it—had long ago given up on Strickland.

"The man is a lost cause," Harry used to say.

"The man is your best customer," I'd respond.

"There's nothing saying he can't be both."

And Strickland probably <u>was</u> the shop's best customer. Over the years, he'd likely purchased more tricks than any two or three magicians in town combined.

The arrival of the Internet and on-line shopping did not appear to slow Strickland down; he lacked the patience to wait for FedEx or UPS to provide the answer he wanted. Nor did he trust the alleged answers provided on YouTube. Our shop was only a short drive away and so—credit card in hand—he'd make the trip and have his answer in mere moments.

It is not uncommon, after a customer purchases a trick, for Harry or me to demonstrate the secret for them (only after cash had exchanged hands, of course). While tricks generally come with written or video instructions, we felt it improved customer relations to help the buyer launch the new trick as quickly as possible. Plus, magic instructions can sometimes be famously opaque.

We'd stopped offering this service for Strickland early on, as it was soul crushing to explain a trick's clever secret and then have the customer merely grunt, nod, and walk out of the store. On more than one occasion, he didn't even bother to take the trick with him.

So, in his case, it was our practice to merely sell him the trick and make him actually have to watch a video or read a sheet of instructions.

"No, I'm not becoming Strickland, not to worry," I said. I could tell I was trying to convince Harry as much as myself. "Eventually, I'll stop thinking about it."

True to my word, I did just that—for about forty-five minutes. And then the sound of the bell over the shop door brought me back to reality.

I pushed my way through the curtain from the back room, expecting to see a familiar face of some kind: a magician-slash-customer, or my friend Nathan, or even the mailman.

Instead, I saw a face that frightened me nearly as much as Mr. Lime's visage.

It was Mr. Lime's assistant. His driver. His who-knows-what-else.

The man he had nicknamed Harpo.

* * *

I THINK I audibly gulped when I saw him standing in the doorway.

He looked the same as he had on the handful of occasions I'd seen him in Mr. Lime's company: A squat and muscular man, the human equivalent of a fireplug, with a neck nearly equal to the width of his shoulders. A tightly trimmed hedge of red hair covered his apparently flat head.

As with all of Lime's movie-themed nicknames, there was a hint of truth to the moniker he'd assigned to the man. He'd called me Mandrake, after the comic book and early movie character; we were both magicians, so that made a certain sense.

In the case of his assistant, the resemblance to the famous comedy film star ended at the fact they were both silent at all times. I'd never noticed any of the warmth or playfulness of Harpo Marx in this man. Just the opposite, in fact. He projected a nearly palpable air of impending violence. His silence only increased that threat ten-fold.

We stared at each other for a long moment. Finally, I asked the question which was hanging in the air between us.

"So, you heard about Mr. Lime?"

He nodded.

Another pause.

"Was it an accident?"

He shook his head

"Do you know how it happened?"

He nodded.

I couldn't figure out how to phrase my next question, and part of me really didn't want to know the answer. But another part did.

"Have you dealt with the person or persons responsible?"

He gave me a long steady look. And then, finally, he nodded.

"I see," I said. "I see."

Now that I had the information, I really didn't know what to do with it. Apparently, someone had killed Mr. Lime and his assistant had extracted a similar, violent revenge. I suppose there were other ways to read that silent answer, but I wasn't seeing them.

Harpo reached into his jacket pocket and I couldn't help it. I flinched.

He very, very slowly removed a white, letter-size envelope from the depths of his coat. He closed the distance between us, holding the envelope out in front of him. It hovered between us for a long, awkward moment. Finally, I tentatively took it from him. The moment I did, he turned and two seconds later he was out the door.

Harry must have heard the bell. He poked his head out between the curtains which separated the back room from the store.

"Who were you talking to out here? Marcel Marceau?"

"It was Harpo," I explained. "Mr. Lime's assistant. Right hand man. Bodyguard. Thug. I don't know."

I weighed the envelope in my hand. Whatever was in there, it wasn't very heavy. Realizing I could easily spend the rest of the afternoon staring at it, I figured it made more sense to just get it over with. I ripped the envelope open like tearing off a Band-Aid. One quick, decisive action.

Inside was a single sheet of paper. I pulled it out and read it once quickly. I whistled slowly, and then read it again.

"What is it? A summons?" said Harry.

I shook my head, still rereading the short missive, reeling a bit from the implications.

"It's from a foundation," I finally said as I handed the sheet to Harry. "This foundation has established a scholarship for fifteen kids to attend a magic convention every year, covering all their costs. My favorite magic convention."

"The Mandrake Scholarship," Harry said slowly. He looked

up at me. "Mandrake the magician? From the comic books? The movie serials?"

I nodded. "That was Mr. Lime's nickname for me. I was Mandrake the Magician. His silent assistant was Harpo. Dylan Lasalle was Francis the Talking Mule. He liked movie-related nicknames."

"So it would seem," Harry said as he looked at the letter again. "Essentially, the scholarship is in your name. It's in honor of you, as it were. But you're the only one who's ever going to know that."

"I think that was by design. I think he wanted to give me something, without actually giving me anything, you know ... overtly."

I headed over to my laptop on the counter, grabbing the letter from Harry as I did. I looked at the name of the foundation in the letterhead and typed it into a search bar. Moments later, I was reading about the foundation and its work.

"Mr. Lime must have set up a foundation, to shelter all of his income after he died. By the looks of this thing, the foundation is only about a month old."

"Well, you can't get much done in a month," Harry commented.

"On the contrary," I said. "If this is legitimate, they seem to be giving money to all sorts of different causes. Clean water, schools, free lunch programs, pre-K education, cancer research. And the Mandrake Scholarship. It goes on and on."

"I thought you said he was a criminal?"

I shrugged. "I got the sense that a lot of what he did was illegal. And that some of it was possibly murderous. And yet, here is a foundation doing all kinds of good things." I looked over at Harry. "If I didn't have any idea who Mr. Lime was before, then I'm completely baffled now."

I stared at the website for a few moments longer and then shut the laptop.

"Let's finish up cleaning out that back room," I said as I pushed my way through the curtains.

* * *

"MAYBE IT WAS like an Ebenezer Scrooge sort of thing," Harry said.

This came out of the blue about thirty minutes later. Although we'd made progress in clearing out the junk—separating the wheat from the chaff—as I glanced around it looked like we'd hardly made a dent. It was becoming clear this was not going to be a one-day job after all.

"What?"

"The transformation your friend went through," Harry said, his voice coming from behind a small tower of cardboard boxes. "Like Scrooge did with The Ghost of Christmas Yet to Come."

"You think Mr. Lime was visited by spirits?"

I could hear Harry grunt in annoyance as he got up. He peered at me over the top of the boxes.

"No, no," he said. "As he got older—like many of us do—he looked back at what he'd done with his life and wanted to change the narrative."

He then launched into what I'm assuming was his Ebenezer Scrooge impression. "Spirit! I am not the man I was. Assure me that I yet may change these shadows by an altered life? Oh, but tell me I may sponge away the writing on this stone!"

"Maybe," I said slowly. "I'm just having trouble merging the two images in my mind: the guy I thought was a total villain suddenly turns out to be generous to a fault."

"Maybe he became generous because of his faults," Harry offered. "He wouldn't be the first, that's for sure. So, you're convinced this Mr. Lime was some sort of an underworld titan?"

I shrugged. "That might be overstating it. But I really got the sense that he was in charge of some sort of criminal syndicate." I pictured the steep stairs leading down to the lake and his final fateful plunge. "Or at least he <u>was</u> in charge. Until recently."

"Sounds like a classic dual reality situation to me."

"Dual reality?"

"Absolutely. You've certainly dealt with that enough in your act. I know for a fact that you do at least one trick that employs dual reality: the volunteer sees one result while the audience perceives something wholly different."

"I'm lost. How does this apply to Mr. Lime?"

"Eli, you live and breathe paradoxes and dual realities on stage, yet seem unable to recognize them in real life," Harry said. "People are not just one thing. Like Kris Kristofferson told us, most of us are partly truth, partly fiction. A walking contradiction."

"You're quoting Kris Kristofferson at me? What's next? Will you offer an insight discovered by The Wichita Lineman?"

"That was Glen Campbell," Harry said as he returned to sorting items from a sagging cardboard box. He looked up as he worked. "There is plenty of precedent. Alfred Nobel invented dynamite but is now only known for the Nobel Prize. Henry Ford was no saint, but he gave us The Ford Foundation. Carnegie. Rockefeller. Vanderbilt. The list goes on and on. Rewriting the narrative. Erasing the past by enriching the future."

I stood there for a long moment, considering this idea, trying to bend my mind around to this new view of Mr. Lime.

Was it possible the worst person I'd ever met was also the best person I'd ever met?

* * *

SNOW HAD FINALLY COME, just in time for Christmas.

Driving was slow and finishing up my final errands had

taken longer than anticipated. My last assignment had been to pick up two focaccia and some herb & garlic mascarpone at Broder's Deli. I wasn't sure why I decided to take the scenic route home until I found myself at the intersection of Penn Avenue and Lake Harriet Boulevard. The steps down to the lake were directly in front of me as I made a right turn. Without even thinking about it, I pulled over and parked, shutting off the car and getting out.

I zipped up my jacket to my neck, wishing I'd brought a hat, as the wind off the lake was sharp and biting. I waited for a snow-covered car to slowly roll past me in the street; the driver had only cleared off the windshield and so the vehicle looked like a slow-moving snowbank. Once it passed, I headed across the street.

The snow was silent beneath my feet, still being in that fresh, fluffy stage. The crunchy phase would come later, when the temperature dropped further. More flakes floated down, visible in the light from the streetlamp, suggesting even more snow was on the way.

A faded wooden barrier had been set across the top of the steps, although it was really just a formality. The steps were dangerous in fine weather; after a couple of snowfalls, you'd have to be insane to attempt them.

I stood at the top of the steep stairway and looked down into the darkness. A dim streetlight was visible by the lake, and the slope of white snow did its best to reflect that light back. But the definition of the steps had been lost in the snowfall. Now it just looked like a scary and badly lit ski run.

I thought back to the early morning phone call from Deirdre and the visit to the morgue. Until the moment I had pulled the sheet back on his corpse, I probably hadn't thought about Mr. Lime for over a year.

Yet over the last month, his name and his image kept popping up in my mind.

Harry had said I was having trouble coming to grips with the paradox of the man's life and I think he was right. I knew Mr. Lime had harmed other people. Probably a lot of other people.

I had slotted him in the bad guy column and let it go at that.

But now I was learning there was more to him than that. It was a lesson which was having trouble adhering to my brain. I don't know why I was resisting it, but I was.

Suddenly my train of thought was interrupted. There wasn't a sound behind me, yet somehow—instinctively—I knew I wasn't alone.

I turned, not sure what I was expecting to see and was utterly surprised by the revelation. And then I saw its inevitability.

It was Harpo.

He was bundled up for the cold, with a heavy coat and a small stocking cap pulled tightly across his wide head.

"Oh," I said as I stepped back. "I didn't hear you come up."

A million thoughts raced through my head, one scenario after another. My first—and strongest—instinct was that it had been Harpo who had pushed Mr. Lime down those thirty-eight steps. And now he was here to do the same with me. I recognized the snowy slope might not kill me, but I was unlikely to walk away from it uninjured.

Harpo merely looked at me and then stepped forward, past me. He stood, looking down into the darkness. He was completely motionless. And then he made the first sound I'd ever heard come out of him.

He sighed.

He turned and looked at me, his face as expressionless as ever.

"You miss him, right?" I said quietly.

He nodded.

"I suppose I do too, in my own way," I said.

We looked down at the white, slippery slope in front of us. Snow continued to fall, the flakes larger than they'd been just a few minutes before.

"I thought I knew who he was," I continued. "Thought I had him all figured out. Thought I was an excellent judge of people. But clearly, I was wrong. In death he was benevolent and thoughtful. Did that come out of the blue? Was he always that way? Did I misunderstand his place in the world, did I misconstrue his actions? Was he a good guy or a bad guy? Or was he both?"

I took a breath. Harpo merely stared blankly back at me.

"I'm not sure why I'm struggling with this to the degree I am," I continued. "I've always known that life is not black and white, that no one is one-hundred percent anything. My biggest nemesis in the magic world, Simon Hartwell, does benefit shows all the time and volunteers at the Children's Hospital. Personally, I think he's a bit of a creep, but you can't deny that's at least a little bit good, right?"

Snow was accumulating atop his stocking cap, but Harpo listened patiently.

"I was thinking about that coin, the quarter," I said. "The police said it was the only thing they had found on him. When did I do that trick for him? Two years ago? Three? I remember it was in a coffee shop, near the magic store. It was snowing then, as well."

Harpo nodded.

"All this time later, and he was still carrying that coin around," I continued. "Of all the things he accumulated in his life, he felt the need to carry that one thing with him. Why was it that important to him? What did it symbolize?"

I looked down the snowy slope in front of us. The stairs, all thirty-eight of them, were entirely obscured.

"I know it's completely self-centered of me—alert the media: a self-obsessed performer—but part of me thinks that maybe, just maybe, I might have made a difference to him. I might have steered him toward this end-of-life beneficence. Maybe something I said or did made an actual difference."

I turned to Harpo. He was still patiently listening. The snow landing on his face was starting to melt, making it look like he was crying. But, of course, that wasn't possible.

"It's a silly thought, I know," I said. "But that's what I keep thinking."

Harpo continued to look at me, without blinking.

And then he did something I'd never expected him to do.

He spoke.

His voice was surprisingly soft and warm. I'm not sure I'd ever had an idea of what he might sound like, but this wasn't it. I guess I thought his voice would be as tough as his demeanor. But it was just the opposite.

"Sometimes people surprise you," he said.

He looked at me for a long moment. He didn't exactly smile, but his scowl appeared to dissolve, if only for a moment.

"Merry Christmas, Eli."

And then, just as he had done in the store, he turned and quickly headed away. He crossed the street and a large car zipped between us. When it had passed, Harpo was nowhere to be seen.

"Merry Christmas," I whispered, wondering—not for the first time—if this encounter had actually taken place.

I stood there for a few minutes more as the snow continued to swirl around me.

And then I headed for home.

THE LAST CUSTOMER

I thought he was going to be my last customer.

Which was a bit ironic, because after a long day in the shop, he was also my first customer. Such is the sad life of a brick-and-mortar magic shop in this day of online browsing and shopping.

At the moment, though, I was in a bit of a fog, trying to decide if the customer's shaggy hair would best be described as dishwater blond or sandy brown. In the midst of what I'm guessing you would call a transaction, the bell over the shop's entrance tinkled. The last customer and I looked at the door as it swung open. For a moment I thought it might have just been the wind, as no one was immediately visible in the doorway. Then I glanced down and saw a kid. He might have been seven or eight or nine or ten—I really have no concept of the standard height-to-age ratio with kids these days. But he looked young.

"We're closed," I said, working hard to take any unintended tone out of my voice.

"The sign in the window says *Open*," the kid said, glancing around the shop, a little wide-eyed at all the magic tricks, posters, and miscellanea that gave Chicago Magic its old-world charm. At least, that's what I chose to think. He also might have been looking at all the clutter and dust.

"I haven't gotten around to flipping the sign," I said. I glanced at the customer to see if this interruption was having any sort of impact on his mood. He seemed as stunned at the kid's moxie as I was.

"Well, then, you're open," the kid said as he stepped further into the shop. "This won't take long, anyway. I need your help and I need it pronto."

The door swung shut behind him, and I exchanged a look with the customer. He nodded a quick assent.

"Okay," I said. "What's the problem?"

The kid took a deep breath. "I need to make a tuba disappear," he said. "Like, now."

I like to think I've heard my share of odd requests in the twenty-plus years I've either helped at the magic shop or run it on my own, but this was a new one. Deep down I knew this moment was not an ideal one for tackling new questions, but I took the kid at his word that this would be a speedy exchange.

"Just how do you mean 'disappear?'" I asked.

"Like this," he said as he pulled out his iPhone. He had a video from YouTube pre-loaded, and he held it up for me to see. The customer leaned in as well.

I recognized the video immediately. It was David Copperfield (the magician, not the Dickens character), pulling off one of his most talked about illusions: making the Statue of Liberty disappear. The pacing of the performance was a whole lot slower than I remembered, but for the television audience—and the small audience watching it live on-site—it was still an impressive feat.

"That's a pretty big effect," I said.

"The tuba's a pretty big instrument," the kid countered.

"Fair point," I agreed. "But before we get into the *how*, maybe it would be best to go over the *why*."

The kid sighed as if he was being forced to repeat previously discussed information to a much older, much dimmer person. He wasn't far off.

"Tomorrow is the talent show at school. Everybody is required to perform in some way. My mom says I have to play the tuba, 'cause of all the money she's been shelling out for lessons."

"Then why don't you just play the tuba?"

"Are you kidding?" he nearly yelped. "A tuba? I'll be laughed off the stage."

"He sort of has a point." This was from the customer, who up until now had been watching this exchange quietly and, I hoped, patiently.

"So, instead," the kid continued excitedly, "I want to come out with the tuba and then make it disappear. Right before their eyes. As if by magic," he added, to ensure I was following his not-too-byzantine thought process.

"Okay, that's a fair premise. How much experience do you have doing magic?"

The kid shrugged. "None, I guess. But it's only one trick," he said confidently. "I figured I could just buy something here to make it happen. Nothing too complicated or expensive," he added. "And nothing too big. I'm already hauling around a tuba."

"Simple to do, not too expensive, and easy to carry around," I summarized quietly. This request was a common one, and sadly not just from neophyte magicians. I was happy, not for the first time today, that my uncle Harry was not manning the shop. It was just this sort of request that would have sent him into an apoplectic fit.

"Well," I said as I processed the request. "A vanish like that requires a lot of control on the part of the magician. You need to manage the audience sight lines, the lighting, the backdrop. In some cases, the construction of the stage itself. Are you likely to have control of any of those factors?"

I assumed these requirements would sound the death knell for his idea, but amazingly, he actually thought it over for several long moments. Finally, he shook his head.

"No, all we get to do is walk out there and perform."

"Well, making the tuba disappear seems to be off the table then."

"Wait—" the kid began, but I held up a hand.

"But that doesn't mean we still can't do something magical," I interjected quickly. "It's just a matter of figuring out what that something might be."

Having faced variations on this question my entire working life, I did what I always did: I crossed the store to a large floor-to-ceiling bookcase that lined one wall of the shop.

"The answer we need is somewhere in here," I said, glancing over my shoulder. The kid had followed me, while the customer stayed by the cash register, his hands still shoved deep into the pockets of his worn and faded Army jacket. From this new vantage point, I decided that his hair color was definitely sandy brown. He stared at me blankly, so I quickly turned back to the task at hand.

The kid stood next to me while I scanned the spines of the books. He looked up at a sign positioned at the top of the bookcase.

"What does '793.8' mean?"

I glanced up at the placard. It had been there for so many years, I had stopped seeing it. Which was odd, given I had been the one to print and post it.

"Well, my uncle Harry has had this habit for years of lending books from the store to magicians rather than selling them outright. In his view, if they don't like the book, they will bring it back. If they do like the book, they will come back and pay for it."

The kid looked up at me doubtfully. "How's that working for him?"

"About how you'd expect," I said. "Which is to say, not well. And since I felt he was turning this into a lending library, I put up that sign. 793.8 is the Dewey Decimal listing for magic books in libraries."

He was looking up at me blankly again, so I continued. "A library is a building where you can borrow books—"

He cut me off. "I *know* what a library is," he snapped. "I'm just surprised that any of them are still using the outmoded Dewey system instead of the far superior Library of Congress classification method."

Now it was my turn to stare blankly at him. "You hear the word *precocious* much?" I finally said.

"Now and again."

"I'm not surprised," I said as I returned my attention to the rows of book options in front of me. "I think what we need is something that makes the tuba the cause rather than the effect. So that there's a reason for the tuba. Otherwise, it will just seem like an unnecessary prop ..."

My voice trailed off as I scanned the titles. Most were on magic theory, while others focused so minutely on specific styles of magic (cards, coins, big-box illusions) that they would be essentially useless in this instance. And then I saw what I was looking for and gave a small cry of inspiration.

"*This* is what we need," I said as I pulled the book off the shelf and read the title out loud. "*Harry's Magic Emporium.*"

I opened the book and began to page through it quickly.

"What's it called?"

The voice surprised me. I turned to see the customer was peering at us from across the room. He had moved away from his position leaning on the counter and was starting to move across the shop.

"Um, it's *Harry's Magic Emporium*," I repeated, splitting my attention between the book and the customer, who was now moving toward us. "My uncle Harry wrote it," I added.

"I remember that book," the customer said, sounding surprised at the memory. "I had it when I was a kid. In addition to the tricks, there were a lot of dumb jokes in it, right?"

"Yes, tons of them. No one loves a bad joke more than my uncle. But, thankfully, no one loves a great trick more than he does either. Now I seem to remember that he organized the book around the thirteen different types of magic, the list he used to argue with Harry Blackstone, Jr., about all the time," I said as I continued flipping through the book.

"There have got to be more than thirteen magic tricks," the kid said, his tone suggesting that he may have wandered into the wrong shop today. On one level he was right, but his statement was off base.

"There are hundreds more," I said. "But they can all be classified into one of thirteen categories. You know, Production, Vanish, Restoration, Animation, Penetration, Transposition . . ."

Just like any time I tried to name all the Seven Dwarfs, I started strong and then petered out about halfway through the list.

"You get the idea," I finally said, still paging through the book in hopes that inspiration would leap from one of the pages. The room was quiet for a few moments, the only sound being paper on paper as I scanned rapidly through the book.

"Do you serve crabs here?"

The question came from the customer and I froze in mid-page turn. I looked over my shoulder at him.

"Excuse me?"

"The patron says, '*Do you serve crabs here?*' And the maître d' says, '*We serve everyone, sir, let me get you a seat.*'" The customer laughed at the joke, shaking his head at the memory. "I thought it was funny long before I understood what it meant."

I nodded in agreement. "I had that same reaction to a lot of Harry's jokes. They were like little joke time bombs, set to go off at a later, unknown date. Like, *Why is six afraid of seven?*"

I looked from the customer to the kid. The kid had no response, but the customer thought for a moment and then laughed.

"*Because seven eight nine,*" he said, smiling for the first time since he'd entered the store.

"This is great," the kid said without inflection. "Big laughs. But can we focus on my disappearing tuba?"

"Right," I agreed, turning my attention back to the book. "I think our best bet would be to use the tuba as a production tool of some kind, sort of like a magician's top hat. Do you have a stand for the tuba?" I asked without looking up from paging through the book.

"Of course I do, the thing is as big as I am," the kid snapped. I got the sense that, to his young mind, I was the stupidest person he had ever met.

"That will help," I said, flipping quickly to the chapter on production.

"Do you only have one copy of the book?"

This was asked by the customer, who had moved again and was now standing silently behind me. I successfully squelched a yelp.

"Nope, Harry has a ton of them," I said, reaching up and pulling another copy off the shelf. I handed it to the customer, who took his hands out of his pockets for the first time as he grasped the book and began to page through it.

"What if we did this," I began, seeing a chapter on silk productions. "What if you came out and started to play, but only got some odd sounds out of the tuba. Like, you know, something was stuck in the horn."

"The bell," the kid said.

"What?"

"It's called the bell. The whole thing is the horn. The part you can reach into is called the bell."

"The bell, whatever. What if that were the premise: you keep trying to play something with the tuba and you get horrible sounds out of it and you keep pulling different odd things out of the horn? The bell."

The kid smiled and nodded. "Sure, that would be fun. But there's limited space in the bell. I mean, there's not as much room as you might think."

"Not a problem, we have ways around that," I said as I handed the book to the kid. "Go to the index and look up *servante*," I said as I turned away and began to scan the products on the shelves.

"What's a *servante*?" the kid asked as he dutifully turned to the back of the book.

"It's a secret way to make things appear and disappear," I said. "Magicians use them all the time."

"Cool," the kid said as he focused on his search.

"Indeed," I said absently. I was looking for items that were designed to pack small and transform to full size with very little effort. I saw a black-and-white cane that would do the trick, pulled it off the shelf, and then reached for a compact bouquet of roses.

"Here's one you'll like," the customer said suddenly. I spun around, but he had his face buried in the book. *"What musical instrument is found in the bathroom?"*

He must have seen that I was busy looking for props, so he turned to the kid and repeated the question, barely able to contain his amusement. *"What musical instrument is found in the bathroom?"*

The kid shrugged. "I don't know."

The customer laughed as he gave the answer, sort of killing

the joke while completing it. *"A tube of toothpaste.* Get it? A tuba toothpaste. You should use that one."

"Sure thing," the kid said flatly, imitating the response of every comedian I've ever met when a lay person offers a joke for their act. "I'll get right on it."

I cut into the conversation, laying out items on a nearby counter. "I don't know the sequence yet," I said as I arranged the ragtag selection of props. "But these are all things you can hide in the horn—sorry, in the *bell*—or in a *servante* we put behind it.

It took a few minutes, but between the kid and me, we structured a short but funny act that involved him pulling an impossible number of items out of the tuba, but still getting poor results every time he blew into the horn. While we worked, the customer leaned against the bookcase, paging through the book in his hands. Every few moments he would let out a small giggle or a yelp of recognition at a re-discovered magic trick or a long-forgotten joke.

"Now we just need a closer," I said as we looked over the props we had assembled. "A final topper."

The kid and I stared at the props, silently willing them to provide the answer we were looking for. The thick silence was broken by the customer.

"What about, what do you call it, one of those things?" he said, holding the book in one hand and gesturing toward his mouth with the other. He began to mime, yanking at his mouth, pulling us both into an impromptu game of charades.

"Taffy?"

"Eating spaghetti?"

"Wax lips?"

He shook his head and then quickly flipped through Harry's book, finally finding the illustration he was looking for: a young man pulling a seemingly endless paper streamer out of his mouth.

"A mouth coil," I shouted, feeling like I'd just won something. "A streamer mouth coil!" I moved behind the counter, trying to remember where we kept them and hoping we hadn't run out.

"That will be great," the kid said, beaming. "I'll let the audience know that the bell is finally empty, then blow into the tuba one last time. I'll still get a horrible sound, and then I'll start pulling the streamer out of my mouth. That will kill. Thanks!"

He looked over at the customer, who was still paging through the book as he walked away from us. The customer looked up, realizing that the compliment had been directed at him.

"No problem," he said to the kid, then he looked at me. "If it's okay, I'll take this book," he said. "I had one as a kid. Loved it. Really loved it."

"Is that all you need?" I asked slowly.

He smiled down at the book. "Yeah, this will do. But," he added, patting his pockets as he glanced at the kid. "I forgot my wallet."

"That's okay," I said, gesturing toward the 793.8 sign over the bookcase. "Remember, this is Harry's lending library."

"Great," he said as he looked back at the book, flipping the pages happily. "Thanks a lot."

He opened and closed the door, his attention still focused on reliving the memories the book was providing. I breathed a deep sigh, but my reverie was short-lived.

"Boy, this looks like a lot of stuff," the kid said slowly, scanning all the items on the counter. "I don't think I can afford all these props."

"Not to worry," I said, gathering them up and starting to load them into a brown paper sack. "On occasion, the lending library concept also extends to magic props," I lied. "And this is one of those occasions."

"Really?" He clearly couldn't believe his good luck. For my part, neither could I.

"Really," I repeated as I walked him to the door. "Come back after the show and let me know how it went."

"And return the props," he added.

"Yes," I agreed, having already forgotten that caveat in the sudden flurry of feelings of relief.

I saw him out the door and turned to head back to the register, where the small bag the last customer had brought still sat by the open cash drawer. I flashed back to that moment—was it only ten minutes ago?—when he had first thrust it at me, demanding the contents of the cash drawer, poking what he said was a gun from the pocket of his worn Army jacket.

I looked down, wiping at the rivulets of sweat that had been running continuously down the back of my neck. Most of the contents of the cash drawer were already in the bag, as he had demanded. The other half was positioned on top of the drawer, ready to follow their compatriots.

I was about to put all the money back in the cash register, when a thought occurred to me. I stepped back to the shop's front door and locked it, turning the deadbolt as well for good measure.

And before I returned to sort out the mess at the cash register and calm my racing heart, I also had the presence of mind to do the one thing I wished I had done thirty minutes earlier. Or an hour. Or right away this morning, before that first —or last—customer walked through my door.

I flipped the sign in the front window with such force that I nearly pulled it off its string hanger.

From *Open* to *Closed*.

Because right now I was many, many things.

But open for business was not one of them.

THE SELF-WORKING TRICK

I

I had jokingly referred to our date as *"Megan and Eli's Dinner and a Murder."*

It wasn't until the end of the second act of the play that I realized just how far-sighted my alleged quip had been.

However, at the moment, I was waiting in giddy anticipation for the big scare I knew was just seconds away. The play was that old classic, *Wait Until Dark*, performed at a local community theater. Because I had provided some nominal magic training to one of the actors in the production, I'd been invited to an early preview to check the quality of my instruction. Having enjoyed that experience—and being in possession of two free tickets for this Opening Night performance—I had suggested the evening as a fun night out, pretty sure that Megan would enjoy the play and (ultimately) the jump scare it offered.

Dinner had been at an Indian restaurant just down the street and although the food was fantastic, the service had been a bit slower than anticipated. Consequently, there was something of a mad rush toward the end of the meal to settle up accounts. This was followed by a quick jog down the street to the theater, which was housed in what clearly had been a church at some point in its history. The sign in front of the building, which in the past had no doubt listed service times, now announced the name of the current play, along with the date for an upcoming fundraising Gala.

We stepped into the building just as the lobby lights were flickering. We were hustled into the auditorium by an agitated usher, who directed us to a fine pair of seats about three rows from the back and dead center. After apologizing our way down the cramped row, we finally sank into our seats and settled back, each a little out of breath, just as the house lights dimmed.

The first act was much like I had seen at the preview earlier in the week, although I sensed the cast had turned up the energy on their performances. This was likely due to the presence of an actual audience. I am intimately familiar with that special shot of adrenaline you get as you're about to step on stage, regardless of whether it's an Opening Night or—in my case—performing my same old magic act for another new audience.

Intermission was spent grabbing a couple of drinks— after a quick trip to the Mens' Room—and then cooling my heels while Megan stood in line, waiting for her turn in the Ladies' Room. I stood patiently in a corner, feeling the two plastic cups of wine in my hands begin to perspire with condensation. Chatter around me centered on reactions to the show, which sounded generally positive. Much adulation was being heaped on the lead actress, particularly praising her believable portrayal of blindness. The actor playing the primary villain was also favorably reviewed, although no mention was made of his character's nervous manipulation of a coin back and forth across his knuckles.

This, it should be noted, had been my sole contribution to the production.

The actor, a charming young fellow named Alex, had wandered into the magic store three weeks earlier, inquiring as to whether or not we offered magic lessons. I confessed that both my uncle Harry and I occasionally took on students, but that we didn't offer anything resembling an official—or, for that matter, structured—curriculum.

That seemed fine with Alex, as he was only looking for instruction on how to roll a silver half-dollar across the backs of his knuckles. In the magic world this is a showy and really pointless piece of magic manipulation, so of course I had spent literally hundreds of hours practicing it. After some questioning, I learned that Alex felt the move would make for a memorable nervous tic for his character. In lieu of payment, he offered a couple tickets to the show. I accepted the proposal and, it being a typically quiet afternoon in the shop, the lesson commenced immediately. Alex was a quick study and he picked up the basics of the handling with surprising speed.

He appeared again a week later to demonstrate his progress on the move and to inquire about a coin routine he had seen on-line. After some questioning on the specifics of what he had witnessed, I deduced he was referring to *Matrix*. This was a coin and card trick developed by fellow Minnesotan Al Schneider, although Uncle Harry would be quick to point out that it was derived from Yank Hoe's *Sympathetic Coins* routine. This was likely due to Harry's insistence on proper crediting on all magic tricks, but also—I think—he was a little peeved that Al Schneider had come up with this classic routine and he hadn't.

I explained a routine like *Matrix* would require actual, formal lessons, as it involved learning a number of specific moves and techniques. I offered my hourly rate, immediately discounted it, and moments later I had a new magic student.

We'd had two lessons since that time and during these two

ninety-minute sessions I learned more about Alex and about the play.

Although not a professional actor, Alex appeared frequently at the theater, the Como Lake Players, as well as at other local community theaters. He was part of what was probably the largest segment of the theater community: non-professionals who didn't get paid but performed simply for the love of it. The magic community has a similar class of performers who don't make their living at the art but are passionately devoted to the craft. Reflecting on the laughable income I made as a quote/unquote Professional Magician, I recognized that most days I was mere inches away from being correctly referred to as a hobbyist.

A casual inquiry from me about how rehearsals for the play were going unleashed an unexpected monologue from Alex. Apparently, it was turning out to be a more-than-usually troubled production. The play's director was indecisive to the point of distraction, constantly changing blocking and driving the costumer and set designer crazy with seemingly endless revisions. To compound that, the other key male role in the show had been cast by an actor who Alex referred to as his nemesis.

"You must have the same thing in your business?" Alex suggested. We were seated in the back of the magic shop, going over his progress on *Matrix*, the table in front of us littered with cards and coins. "You know, someone who always seems to get the better gig, again and again."

I nodded along, recognizing immediately that I did, in fact, have a nemesis in the magic community: Simon Hartwell.

For years, Simon had nearly always seemed to get the bigger and better gigs, leaving me—in my mind—to paw through the dregs. In reality, of course, he wasn't really doing all that much better. Simon was simply more adept at announcing his engagements on Facebook and Instagram, each post making me feel my career was quickly disappearing into a murky bog.

"And then, this week, a new bombshell," Alex continued. "Our lead actress suddenly quit."

"Conflicts with your indecisive director?" I suggested.

"No, the traitor went over to the dark side," Alex explained. "She got a last-minute paying gig at The Guthrie."

"Wow. How do you go about fixing that? Doesn't the play open in about ten days?"

Alex nodded. "Normally, it would be an unmitigated disaster," he said. "However, as luck would have it, the theater's Executive Director played the same role three years ago in summer stock. So, after considerable coaxing, Leah's agreed to step into the part."

"Lucky for the play, but that's got to be a headache for her."

"She had to do the same thing once before, right after she joined the theater," he said. "She swore she'd never do it again."

"Never say never," I offered.

"Hey, that's exactly what I said to her," Alex said with a grin before returning his attention to the four coins on the table in front of him.

* * *

"This theater is in desperate need of extra restrooms."

I looked up to see that Megan had joined me. I handed her the remaining full plastic cup of wine; mine had long been emptied. "I don't know, I was in and out of the Mens' Room in no time at all."

The kick she directed at my ankle may have been playful, but it was also sharp and effective.

"Yes," I continued. "You are absolutely correct. It's a terrible injustice."

Before I could dig myself out of this hole any further, the

lobby lights flashed, signaling the intermission was drawing to a close. Megan quickly consumed the contents of her cup. I deposited it, along with my empty, in the recycling bin as we joined the throng slowly wending its way back into the auditorium.

I spent the whole of the second act in anticipation of the jump scare I had received at the preview earlier in the week. It's a classic moment I remembered from the movie version of *Wait Until Dark*, but I had forgotten about it while watching the preview.

The director, for all of his or her faults, had staged it beautifully: The set was pitch black, lit only by light coming from an open refrigerator. The blind heroine who has, apparently, killed the villain, is making her way clumsily toward the apartment's front door. Then, suddenly, out of the blackness a figure lunges at her.

This surprise—the sudden and homicidal appearance of the not-as-dead-as-you-thought-he-was villain—produced the intended effect on the audience: They screamed as one, the auditorium vibrating as two hundred people simultaneously jumped in their seats. As I had anticipated, Megan leapt higher than most, at the same time letting out a surprised and sustained yelp. Megan's was not the only scream inspired by this jump scare, but since she was sitting next to me, it sounded like the loudest.

But surprisingly, it was quickly replaced by a louder scream, which was coming from somewhere behind me. The action of the play continued, as the heroine and the villain struggled on-stage, but for some unknown reason, the scream behind me continued. In fact, it sounded like it was getting louder and louder. People began to turn and peer in the dark toward the painful sound. It persisted unabated until finally the action on the stage came to a stop and the actors, along with most of the audience, turned toward the back of the theater.

After much rumbling and calls for 'Lights, lights, turn on the lights," the houselights finally popped on. And then we were all able to see what all the screaming was about.

A woman in the back row was standing, her hands covering her mouth, although this action was doing precious little to muffle her screams. Her shrieks were soon combined with a chorus from nearby theatergoers, as we all saw what had frightened her so badly.

The man seated next to her was slumped forward. He was clearly dead, and the cause was in plain view: A large knife had been plunged cleanly into the center of his back.

2

ODDLY ENOUGH, I've become something of an old hand at homicide investigations, so nothing which followed really surprised me.

Multiple simultaneous 911 calls by various audience members summoned uniformed officers almost immediately. The police locked down the location and were joined a few minutes later by two homicide detectives. The crime scene was cordoned off and we were directed out of the auditorium, the large crowd filling up both the front lobby and the much larger back lobby.

It was fortunate the theater's Executive Director was on-hand, since she also happened to be playing the lead in the play. She conferred with the homicide detectives while still dressed in her show costume and make-up. It quickly became apparent that she was completely in charge of this peculiar situation and also not—in fact—blind.

"It's a ticketed event," she was explaining to the detectives when I got close enough to hear. "We have the phone numbers, email addresses and credit card information for all ticket buyers, and we know where each party was seated, so we can get you all that data. Plus, the front and back doors are locked during performances, so while it's possible that someone might have left after the, um, crime, it's unlikely anyone other than audience members were in the building when it happened."

"And the cast and crew, of course," added an older woman who appeared to work at the theater. I think I had seen her in the box office when Megan and I had made our whirlwind rush through the lobby just before the show started. The older woman turned to the lead detective and poked him in the arm. I got the sense they had crossed paths before.

"I've pulled the CCTV footage from the back and front door," she continued. "Those cameras are motion-sensitive. I did a quick check. Nothing was recorded after the smokers came back into the building at the end of Intermission."

"We'll need copies of that," the detective said.

"Ready whenever you need it," the old woman replied quickly.

She headed back toward the box office as the detective turned to one of the uniformed officers. "There's no point keeping all these people here," he said. "Start letting people go, just make sure you get IDs on everyone before they leave."

The cop nodded and immediately started to work, herding people toward the front door. In short order, Megan and I were in line to leave, and several minutes later we were out on the street.

3

"You told me the play had a surprising ending, but I think you undersold it," Megan said as we stopped on the sidewalk in front of the theater. "You'll have to tell me the real ending at some point."

I noticed a bar/restaurant across the street called Jimmy's. "It's still early," I said. "Let's grab a drink and a snack and I'll enthrall you with the actual but somewhat less compelling ending to *Wait Until Dark*."

Other theatergoers had clearly had the same idea, because the hostess said it would be several minutes before a table might open up. She offered bar seating in the interim, which was fine with us. All we were looking for were two seats together.

We found those two stools at the end of the bar and at the same time spotted a recognizable face: Alex, my new magic student, was just grabbing a pitcher of beer from the bartender.

"Quite a show, huh?" he said with a weary shake of his head once we were within speaking range. "That will be tough to top next weekend."

I agreed and introduced Megan.

"You were really scary," she said after a quick handshake. "But you seem nice up close."

"That's what it says at the top of my resume," Alex said. "Scary at a distance, nice up close." He was holding the pitcher of beer with one hand while grasping for a bowl of pretzels on the bar. I reached out and grabbed the salty snack for him.

"You want to join us in the back, we have a couple extra seats?" he said, indicating with a quick nod where "in the back" was located. I looked at Megan. Although there were two perfectly acceptable stools at the bar, the area was dense with televised sporting events and highly vocal fans. She gave me her best "yes please!" expression.

"Lead the way," I said to Alex as I grabbed a second bowl of pretzels for sustenance during the short journey.

The faces at the cozy table looked oddly familiar, if slightly out of context. Having spent the evening watching them on stage (as well as at the preview earlier in the week), it was strange seeing the cast seated at a corner table, wearing different clothes and attitudes.

Alex made some quick introductions, and I did my best to capture and hold onto the names before his words disappeared into the ether. From years of pulling people on-stage for my act, I've developed the short-term skill of remembering names for the duration of a routine; however, hanging onto those names beyond that short time span still often eludes me.

Alex poured himself a beer from the pitcher before handing it around the table. We were one chair short, so I gestured Megan toward the remaining seat and then found another chair at a nearby table.

"Are we expecting others?" I asked Alex as I pulled the chair over and settled in. I looked around the room for other available chairs and also—more importantly—in hopes of spotting a waitress.

He shook his head. "Leah said she'd come over after the police leave, but I doubt that will be anytime soon. We were supposed to be at an Opening Night party right now, but clearly that's not happening."

This comment produced sounds of agreement from the other actors.

"Yep, this was certainly an Opening Night for the record books."

This came from the young man across the table from me, who I recognized as the good-guy-who-turns-out-to-be-the-bad-guy in the play. He had introduced himself as Lloyd Williams and I sensed immediately he was probably the nemesis Alex had talked about earlier; they were both about the same age and physical type, and I could imagine them going head-to-head at auditions.

Next to him was the actress who played the teenage neighbor in the play. She said her name was Gloria something; her last name disappeared into the general hubbub of the bar.

The first thing I noticed was she clearly wasn't actually a teenager. While she gave that impression on-stage, up close even in dim bar lighting it was evident she was pushing thirty and maybe even from the other side. However, she was small and slight and had pulled off the role with aplomb.

She handed the almost empty pitcher to the actor next to her, who played one of the other heavies in the play. He introduced himself just as Omar, so I was spared trying to remember yet another surname. Omar was heavyset and balding, and I wondered for a moment if the director had cast him due to his slight resemblance to Jack Weston, the actor who had played the same part in the movie version of *Wait Until Dark*. Like Weston, Omar possessed a slick charm, which worked well for him on-stage. He had been one of the best actors up there and I was sorry his character had been one of the first to die.

Omar drained the pitcher into his glass and, for some reason, handed the now-empty container across the table to the actor who had played the blind woman's husband. I struggled for a moment to pull the name I had heard twenty seconds before. After several moments of nothingness, it finally came to me: Tom Drake. He looked at the empty pitcher for a long moment and then slowly stood up.

"I guess the next round is on the newbie," he said with a grim chuckle as he began to head toward the bar.

"That's right," Gloria said with a laugh. "And, if you need any help, the bar is stage left, upstage from where you are now."

She laughed heartily at the jab, and the other actors joined in, but to a lesser degree. Tom gave this remark a sad smile as he headed toward the bar.

I turned to Megan. "Looks like if we want anything, we have to order it from the bar," I said. "You hungry?"

Megan shook her head. "No, I'll just take a Coke and some nachos," she said, and then added quickly. "Oh, and maybe some onion rings. With ranch dressing."

I stood up to follow Tom Drake to the bar but was stopped by Gloria's piercing voice behind me. She certainly knew how to project.

"Hey, grab me a vodka tonic while you're up, would ya?"

I nodded to indicate my willingness for the task, but she had already turned away and was deep in conversation with Omar.

I wove my way through the crowd and moments later joined Tom at the bar. He had already summoned the bartender's attention and his pitcher was in the midst of being filled. He turned to me and we nodded.

"A newbie, huh?" I said, searching for some common ground on which to establish what would likely be a brief conversation.

"Yeah, this is my first play," he said. Although he had seemed quite confident on-stage as the blind woman's husband, he now seemed nervous and self-aware. I was familiar with this incongruous duality; many of the brashest magicians I knew were wallflowers off-stage.

"Well, you looked like a pro to me," I said.

"Thanks, I'm still trying to find my feet," he said quickly. He glanced over his shoulder at the waiting table. "I guess I just need to get a few more shows under my belt."

"A life in the theater," I said, sounding way too jovial.

Before Tom could respond, the bartender pushed the now-full pitcher toward him. Tom deposited some cash on the bar and disappeared into the crowd. At the same time, I tried to recapture the bartender's attention. After three attempts, I was able to place my drink order.

"Can I order food here as well?" I asked.

"Sure, looks like your waitress has her hands full. What can I get you?"

I put in the order for the nachos and onion rings, with a side of ranch dressing. I was about to head back to the table with our two Cokes when I remembered Gloria's last-minute request for a vodka tonic.

Moments later I was navigating my way through the crowd, balancing the three slippery drinks. I placed Megan's in front of her, then slid the vodka tonic across the table toward Gloria. It was then I noticed she was conversing—quietly but heatedly— with a guy who had approached the table. He looked down and saw the new drink in front of her.

"Another drink? I thought we were going to make it an early evening?" he said, no longer speaking softly.

"It is still early," Gloria snapped. "Why don't you go back and watch more of your sports ball stuff?"

"The game's over and I'm tired," he growled. He looked to be a little older than her, well-dressed with just the beginnings of grey around his temples. "Let's go."

He turned to go, got a few steps and looked back. Gloria was not following him. He gave her a stern look and she reluctantly stood and approached him. This was followed by a harsh but whispered conversation between the two. After several moments of discussion, Gloria returned to the table.

"I can have this last drink," she said, all the energy gone from her voice. "And then hubbie says it's pumpkin time for me."

With that, Gloria picked up the drink and turned her attention back to a conversation with Omar. Her husband leaned against a wall and turned his attention to one of the bar's many television screens, while still making occasional cold glances in our direction.

"Thanks for the Coke," Megan said quietly.

I felt bad leaving her at a table full of strangers. "No problem, food is on the way. So, did I miss anything?"

She shook her head. "You know how magicians basically always have the same three conversations?"

"Why aren't I working, why is he working, and why isn't there any work?" I offered.

Megan nodded. "Turns out, actors do the same thing."

"How lucky for you that you get to hear variations on these themes wherever you go."

She gave me a quick smile and then we turned to listen to the actors as they revisited the evening's performance and their theories about its sudden interruption.

Moments later our food arrived. Megan and I graciously shared the appetizers with the table, consequently getting far less than we might have liked. I noticed Gloria was really making her drink last, despite occasional annoyed glares from her husband.

I was considering another trip to the bar for a repeat of the nachos when I glanced over and saw Williams had produced a deck of cards.

"Since Alex is in the midst of taking magic lessons from Eli here, but refuses to demonstrate anything except that silly coin across the knuckles," Williams said, his volume turned up to performance mode. "I thought I'd show you folks a real card trick. It's done with just twenty-one cards."

Megan looked over to see how well I was holding back my true feelings and, judging by her reaction, I must have been producing a relatively decent poker face.

It's always been a mystery to me as to why people insist on performing card tricks in front of magicians. Maybe I'm a snob, but if you were at a dinner party with a dermatologist, would you point out moles on your fellow guests and attempt to out-diagnose the good doctor? Insist on showing Billy Joel your superior version of *Piano Man*? Challenge Marcel Marceau to a game of Charades?

And why was it always *The Twenty-One Card Trick*?

I glanced at Alex and he returned my look with a pained expression of his own. While I'm sure he was carrying the pieces he needed to perform *Matrix*—it only requires a few coins and four cards—we both knew he wasn't ready to try it out on an actual audience. I silently applauded his restraint. It was a lesson I had learned from my first days in magic. My uncle Harry would often work on a new routine for upwards of a year before he'd let anyone, even me, see it in action.

"Can I see what you're working on?" I might ask Harry in passing.

"Oh, heavens no Eli," my uncle would say with a chuckle. "It's not anywhere near ready for public consumption."

While I wasn't being that strict with my student, as a performer Alex recognized he still needed more rehearsal and practice before he would be ready to successfully perform his new routine to the world at large.

"Twenty-one cards are all we need," Williams continued after he'd culled that number from the full deck. And then he was off and running.

Or, more to the point, off and counting.

After Gloria secretly looked at one of the twenty-one options presented to her, Williams then started dealing out the cards, face up, into three stacks. The object was for Gloria to identify which stack held her chosen card, without revealing its actual identity. Williams then re-assembled the cards and started the dealing process all over again. Déjà vu, but not in a fun way.

There are performers who can make this trick work. I was thinking notably of Bill Malone, whose version is a delight. But Lloyd Williams was no Bill Malone. He dealt the cards way too slowly, making three unnecessarily neat piles and dragging the process out to twice its required length.

Then disaster struck. And Williams was completely unaware.

It happened when he looked up while dealing and said,

"Hey Alex, I can show you how this is done later. Not to worry, anyone can do it. It's self-working."

He said this with a wink and a sneer and returned his attention to the three stacks in front of him, unaware he had miscounted the second stack. I wondered if I should alert him to this misstep but realized—as Uncle Harry liked to say—this wasn't my circus and these weren't my monkeys. Plus, I hadn't cared for the passive-aggressive tone in his crack to Alex about the trick being self-working.

And so, like the others, I watched as Williams went through the dealing process one last time and then prepared to announce which card was the one Gloria had chosen. But unlike the others, I already knew he would be wrong. Plus, I also knew the true location of the desired card.

Trust me on this: Few things in this world fizzle out more anticlimactically than a long and botched card trick. When Williams revealed the card and Gloria denied it was hers, what little energy remaining at the table evaporated in a quick puff of sad, disappointed smoke.

Of course, since I knew where the correct card was, I could have easily saved Williams. I could have turned the trick into a two-hander and with some clever patter revealed the correct card to much enthusiasm and applause. Taking it a step further, with very little effort I could have produced the anticipated card from my own pocket. I had a deck of cards on me and—without revealing how—I knew exactly where the King of Spades was located within it. I could have saved the trick, and Williams, and brought the routine to a rousing conclusion.

But I did none of that.

Instead, I let Williams simmer in his wrongness, annoyed that he'd attempted—and botched—a simple trick, and more annoyed that he had unnecessarily belittled my student in the process.

Attention on Williams' moment of shame was suddenly

diverted by the breathless appearance of the show's lead actress, Leah. She had changed out of her costume and seemed winded by the short trek from the theater to the bar. All eyes turned away from the sad display of cards in front of Williams to this new arrival.

"Are you done with the police?" Alex asked.

I glanced around for an additional chair, although I realized I could simply offer her my own; I was getting the sense from Megan that she'd like to head out sooner rather than later. Gloria's husband had stepped up to the table and it looked like —if he had his way—his wife's chair would also be available in a matter of moments.

"The police are still there, but Betsy said she'd lock up after them," Leah said. "But wait until you hear this: You know what the murder weapon was?"

If people hadn't been interested in Leah's arrival before, they were riveted now. Alex shook his head.

"It was the knife for the Opening Night cake," Leah said. "It had been on display all evening in the back lobby, right next to the cake."

"Talk about a crime of opportunity," Alex said with a low whistle. "Anyone could have grabbed it during Intermission."

"But that's not the weirdest thing," Leah continued. "I overheard a couple of the cops and found out who got stabbed."

She gave her impending pronouncement a dramatic pause before uttering the victim's name.

"It was Jeremy McCormick."

The name meant nothing to me, but it was clearly familiar to the actors seated around the table. The announcement produced a hubbub of chatter. Gloria yelped. Omar sat back in his chair like he'd been punched in the chest. Tom Drake, who had been pale before, started to look a bit gray.

But I couldn't help notice that, amidst the commotion, Alex

and Lloyd Williams merely exchanged an apprehensive look. And then immediately turned away from each other.

4

"YOU KNOW THAT EXPRESSION, 'The enemy of my enemy is my friend?'"

I nodded. "I'm familiar with it."

"Well, it's not always correct," Alex continued. "Sometimes, the enemy of my enemy is also my enemy. And that's a pretty apt description of my relationship with Jeremy McCormick. And Lloyd Williams felt the same way as well."

We were seated in the back room at Chicago Magic, once again working on *Matrix*. Alex was really coming along on the routine, so today's session consisted mostly of honing and sanding off a few of the rougher edges.

"So, you're saying both you and Williams had a contentious relationship with the murder victim?"

"We didn't like each other and weren't shy about it," Alex said. "Jeremy was a creep and a liar and a backstabber."

We exchanged a quick look. "Backstabber?" I repeated.

"Maybe not the best choice of words," Alex agreed.

"Maybe not. But, from the police point of view, I would have to think your shared dislike of the victim was hardly enough motivation to murder him."

"Exactly. Plus, don't forget, we were both on stage at the time. Dead on stage, for that matter."

"Well, Williams was dead," I corrected. "You weren't as dead as the audience thought you were."

"True enough, but I <u>was</u> onstage."

"Given that, do you think the police really suspect you? Or Williams for that matter?"

Alex shook his head. "Not seriously. They had me come

down and talk to them for about thirty minutes. But I got the sense they were just going through the motions. Mostly they asked me about other people who had relationships with Jeremy. I told them he's been in the theater scene for years. I bet even Gloria had a short fling with him at one point."

"Before she was married?"

Alex shrugged. "It's hard to tell with Gloria. She's one of those actors who always stirs up a relationship in every show she does. You can count on it like clockwork. Plus, I think her view on marriage vows is that they're merely suggestions. And not hard and fast rules."

Alex set down the cards he'd been handling and began to stretch his fingers, trying to loosen them up. "But that doesn't really matter: Gloria was backstage, waiting to come on. I could see her and Tom Drake standing in the wings."

"But her husband was also there, right? At that performance?"

Alex nodded. "Yep. He was on the other side of the aisle from where the murder took place."

"Well, if Gloria had a thing with Jeremy at some point, maybe her husband stabbed him. Jealously is a pretty good motive. The knife was there in the lobby. And he was just across the aisle from the guy."

"Not likely," Alex said. "First, if Gloria's husband is going to start stabbing guys she's slept with, he's gonna need to purchase a twenty-four-piece cutlery set. Maybe a couple of them. But more importantly, his seat wasn't on the aisle. He was like four seats in. So how could he crawl out of his spot without being noticed?"

I remembered how tight the squeeze had been when Megan and I tried to get to our seats before the show started, banging the knees of several people who were already nestled in our row.

"What about Omar?" I suggested.

Alex considered this idea. "The police asked me the same thing. I'm not sure if Omar had any relationship with Jeremy. But he <u>was</u> all alone downstairs in the green room when it happened."

"So, he had opportunity," I said.

"And the means, since everyone knew the knife was out there, just waiting to cut the Opening Night cake," Alex added. "I just don't see a motive for Omar."

We sat quietly for several seconds, and then I decided it was time to turn our attention to the lesson. First up, I had Alex go through the whole routine, top to bottom, to see the moments which needed work. Although he was doing a stellar job for a newbie, I noted several places where he'd benefit from more precise direction.

"The problem with that one moment," I said after we'd finessed a couple of the earlier issues, "is that you're working very hard to make it look like you're doing nothing at that moment."

"I know," he agreed. "It looks odd, but I can't put my finger on why."

"Well, it looks and feels odd because you <u>should</u> be doing something right there," I explained. "That's because you've done something right there at every other point in the trick. There is, by design, a lot of repetition in *Matrix*. So, by not doing the same thing you've done all along, you're drawing attention to it."

I picked up the full deck of cards to demonstrate. "For example, if throughout a trick I'm dealing like this and then, out of nowhere, I deal one card in a slightly different way, it will stand out in the audience's minds," I said. "You've unknowingly created a pattern and then you've broken it. The audience may not know what you did, but they recognize that *something* is different."

We spent several minutes working on options for that

moment, to make it look as natural as possible.

"It's harder than it looks," Alex said, his frustration clearly evident in his voice.

"That's true of many of the best moments in magic," I replied. "Jugglers want the audience to see how hard they're working, while we magicians do just the opposite. If they can see the effort, it literally takes the magic out of the moment."

"Maybe I should stick to self-working tricks," Alex mused. He looked over at me. "What is a self-working trick, anyway?"

"It's a unicorn," came a voice from the other side of the curtain which separated the back of the store from the shop itself. It was Uncle Harry, who had clearly been listening in on our lesson. He pushed his way through the drape.

"No trick is truly self-working, that's just advertising hype," Harry continued as he ambled over to our worktable. It had been a quiet morning in the shop; the last time the bell over the front door rang had been when Alex arrived for his lesson.

"Every trick requires one thing, regardless of how simple it might be," he went on. "It requires a performance."

Although I don't think he noticed, I mouthed the last word as Harry said it. This was a sentiment I'd heard from my uncle my entire life.

"So, like The Twenty-One Card Trick," Alex began, but Harry cut him off.

"It has to be performed," Harry snapped. "Every trick—whether it requires fancy sleights or the not-so-impressive art of counting—requires a performance on the part of the magician. That's why he—or she—is called a *performer*."

"Sure," Alex said. "But that trick was ninety-percent counting. Which is, intrinsically, boring."

"Is it?" Harry said, a hint of challenge in his voice. He had already pulled a small packet of cards out of his vest pocket. He began to count the cards. "Let's see here, I have one, two, three, four, five, six cards in this packet. I place one, two, three of the cards on the table, leaving me with how many cards?"

"Three," Alex said quickly.

"Let's just see," Harry continued as he counted through the packet again. "I have one, two, three, four, five, six cards in this packet. I place one, two, three of the cards on the table. How many cards do I have now?"

"Three?" Alex offered with no confidence.

"Let's just see," Harry said as he counted out the cards in his hand. "I have one, two, three, four, five, six cards in this packet. I place one, two, three cards on the table ..."

Harry continued through the short routine, frying Alex's brain while dramatically demonstrating his point. He reached the end of the trick—his version of a popular illusion called *Six Card Repeat*.

"Counting doesn't have to be boring," he said. "And if it is, I blame the magician and not the trick."

"But what if you can't even get the counting right?" I offered, remembering Williams' rookie mistake at the bar.

"Well, then you probably shouldn't be doing the trick in the first place," Harry replied sharply as he scooped up the pile of cards and headed back to the shop.

Alex waited a few seconds after Harry had disappeared and then turned to me. "How did he do that?"

"That's a lesson for another day," I said. I gestured to the cards and coins in front of us. "Let's stay focused."

"Speaking of another day," Alex said. "I have a favor to ask."

"Shoot."

"It's really more for Leah and the theater," he continued. "The big annual fundraising Gala is coming up and we're short one Emcee. The guy who was doing it *pro bono* has flaked out on her. Apparently, he got a paying gig."

"Not very professional on his part," I said. "And you'd like me to step in and save the day?"

"Something like that," Alex agreed.

"Let me check my calendar, but I'm on-board in principle." I pulled my phone out to check my availability for that date. "Who bailed on you, if you can say?"

"I'm not sure if this is good news or bad news," he began.

"Don't tell me," I said as I held up my hand. "Simon Hartwell."

"Exactly," Alex said with a wince.

"What a putz," I muttered. "Tell Leah I'm in. Now let's get back to work."

5

"THANKS FOR DOING THIS, for free and on such short notice," Leah said quickly as she ushered me into the theater's lobby.

"No problem," I said. "I have a surprising history of stepping into Simon Hartwell's shoes after he's found a pair which he finds more attractive." I wasn't particularly pleased with the metaphor, but I seem to have gotten my point across. Leah was nodding along.

"I know what you mean. I've had to do it twice here at the theater—stepping into major roles at the last minute both times—and I'm hoping not to make a habit of it."

"Well, you were terrific in *Wait Until Dark*," I said. "Has the media attention around the murder had an impact on the show?"

"As terrible as it sounds, we saw a big bump in sales right away," she said. "We'd like to extend the run, but we have another show in rehearsal and if we extend one show, it will throw off the calendar for the rest of the year. Such is the downside of success at the community theater level."

We had reached the double doors which led into the auditorium. The first set were open, while the inner set of doors were closed. I could hear voices coming from within.

"I don't know if Alex fully explained the structure of our Gala show," Leah said as we stopped by the outer doors. "It's a preview of our next season, so the audience gets to see snippets of each of the nine plays. Each piece runs about five minutes. It can make for a sort of disjointed evening, I'm told, but that's what they've done historically."

"And I'm the glue that holds it all together?"

"With any luck, yes," Leah said with a grin. "It was my idea to have a professional host. When we booked Simon Hartwell, we came up with the theme "The Magic of Theater." Hokey, I know, but that's what happens when committees make decisions."

"Not a problem, you should hear some of the corporate themes I've had to work with," I said. *"Together We're Better, In It To Win It, Pride & Performance,"* I rattled off quickly. "My favorite was *A Collection of Bright Stars Does Not A Galaxy Make.* It's been years and I'm still trying to figure that one out."

Leah laughed. "Anyway, your job is to simply welcome the audience, maybe do some tricks between acts, and introduce each play segment. Did you get the script I emailed over?"

I held up the stapled sheets I'd printed out that morning. "It all seems pretty straightforward," I said. "I've made some notes on some possible opening effects, some interstitial stuff that sort of ties into each play segment, and then a nice finale."

"It sounds like you've done more work on this than I have," Leah said with a laugh. She listened at the door for a second. The sound of voices within had faded. "Let me just see how far they are on the tech rehearsal and then we'll get you in and walk through your segments."

"No problem," I said. "Take your time, I'm in no hurry."

With a nod of thanks, Leah headed into the theater. I stood by the closed doors for a few moments and then began to wander around the lobby. I was drawn to a photo display on one wall, which upon inspection turned out to be headshots of the cast of *Wait Until Dark*.

I was reminded immediately of my first headshot when I'd gotten into magic on what was, at best, a semi-professional level. The pose I had picked could have been from just about any cookie-cutter magician out there at the time: It was me, with bad hair and a too-large tuxedo, grinning as I fanned a deck of cards toward the camera. The memory made me wince. I wondered, not for the first time, if the headshot had lost me more work than it got me.

I scanned the photos. Alex grinned brightly at the camera, while Lloyd Williams had struck a more serious tone. Gloria didn't look like a teenager in her photo, just like in real life. I was still surprised at how she had pulled off that transformation on-stage. Tom Drake looked a little wide-eyed, like the photographer had caught him by surprise. Omar stared back at me without expression. And then there was Leah's headshot, which I noticed immediately was slightly different from the others. The lighting was not the same and the background, although similar, didn't match.

"They pulled her photo from another show," said a voice behind me. I turned to see it was Omar, looking at me with the same, blank expression he'd had in his photo. "Because she joined us late in the process. She wasn't there when our show headshots were taken."

I nodded a greeting and turned back to the display.

"A motley crew," Omar continued, moving so that he was now standing alongside me. "Better than some, worse than others."

"You've done a lot of shows here?" I asked, not sure if I was just making conversation or if I was digging for something deeper.

Omar shrugged. "A few. When they need a fat guy. Or a bald

guy. Or a fat, bald guy. With a little warning, I can even give you a fat bald guy with a beard." He turned and grinned at me.

"Character actors never die?" I suggested.

"Damn straight."

I decided I was, in fact, digging. So, I continued.

"Alex said the police questioned him. About the murder. And that they talked to you, as well."

"Yes, that was a new one for me," Omar said with a slow shake of his head. "I mean, they were nice enough about it. And I can see their point: After Gloria and Tom left the green room to go upstairs for their final scene, I <u>was</u> all alone. So, it makes sense to think I might have gone up to the lobby, grabbed the knife and done the deed while everyone else was on-stage. But the fact is, there's just no motive. I mean, I knew Jeremy, but just barely."

"Had you ever been in a show with him?"

"Years ago, and we didn't even have scenes together."

"Someone mentioned that maybe he'd been involved with Gloria at some point?" This had started out as a statement but evolved into a question by the time I got to the end of the sentence.

"Who knows, there's no shortage of those guys. Although," he added as he turned to me, "Gloria might be outgrowing that. I've been in plenty of shows with her and this is the first time, to my memory, she hasn't had a serious fling with another cast member. You used to be able to set your watch to her."

"That's interesting," I said. I decided to press further. "Even you?"

Omar laughed. "Hardly. Gloria doesn't ride my bus. For a while, I thought she might have set her sights on the new guy, Tom. But that didn't seem to go anywhere."

"Alex also said that both he and Lloyd Williams had a contentious relationship with Jeremy McCormick over the years."

Omar laughed. "That was no secret. But they were both on-stage at the time, so how do they make that happen?"

"How indeed."

"Here's my theory and I wasn't shy about telling it to the police: I think someone snuck in during Intermission, making their way into the building with the smokers. Then, they hid in the Mens' room, waiting for that scene when the theater goes entirely dark. They grabbed the knife, stabbed Jeremy, and hightailed it back to the Mens' room until the lobby filled up."

"That's a thought," I said. "What did the police think?"

"The detective I talked to made some notes, but I don't think he was buying it."

"Well, if your theory is correct, the killer needed to have some pretty specific knowledge about the play and the theater," I offered as I walked toward the doors to the auditorium. "I mean, they had to know it would be pitch black in there long enough to get in, stab Jeremy and get out. They needed to know that the two sets of doors would allow them to get in without light spilling in from the lobby. And, to me the biggest question: They had to know where Jeremy was sitting and be able to find him in the dark."

"Yeah, I was wondering about that, too. If Alex or Williams were involved—which I don't think they were—they might have been able to spot him and see where he was sitting during Act One. But, again, they were on-stage when he was killed, along with Leah. Gloria and Tom were right off-stage, waiting to go on. I was in the Green Room."

His voice trailed off. "Perhaps it was suicide," he finally said with a laugh. "Or maybe Jeremy hired a hit man to knock him off. That's a popular trope in movies, isn't it? The guy who hires someone to kill him?"

"Sure thing," I agreed. "But I don't think it comes up that often in real life."

"Too bad, that would have been a clean solution," Omar

said. "So, are you here for the tech rehearsal?" He nodded toward the closed double doors.

I nodded. "Yep, I'm your new Emcee. You're in the show?"

"Just barely," he said. "Jeremy was supposed to perform in one of the scenes. Now that he's not available, I was asked to step in."

"A good part?" I asked, trying to sound as casual as possible. But Omar was on to me.

"An okay part, I guess," he said, grinning. "But not worth killing for."

Before I could press this point further, Leah popped her head through the closed double doors.

"Eli, we're ready for you," she said.

I nodded a goodbye toward Omar and followed her into the auditorium. I turned just as the doors started to swing shut and saw that he was still watching us. He continued to stare until the closing doors silently obscured him from view.

6

"I'M SORRY," I said, turning toward Leah. "What did you say?"

I hadn't heard her because, once we stepped into the auditorium, my attention had immediately turned to the seat in the back row where Jeremy McCormick had been sitting when he'd been stabbed.

I think I expected to see the area cordoned off with yellow police tape. However, if that had been the case earlier in the week, it was no longer an official crime scene. Instead, as I turned to my left as we made our way down the center aisle, I simply saw a line of matching seats that made up the theater's last row. It was identical to the row on my right. No sign of recent homicidal activity.

"I was saying," Leah repeated, "that we'll just go through

your cues, in order. No need for you to be here for the cue-to-cue for all nine of the scenes."

"That's great," I said as we neared the stage. I glanced up to see the set for *Wait Until Dark*, looking slightly less dynamic under the bright work lights. Leah directed me toward a temporary stair unit, which had been added to the far end of the stage.

"There isn't money in the budget to take down the current set for the Gala," she explained as I followed her up the steps. "So, it's traditionally performed on the set of whatever show is running. They tell me the year they did it during the run of *Marat/Sade* made for a particularly grim event, although for some reason it brought in a ton of money."

I followed her to center stage and looked out into the house. Even from this distance, with more lights on me than were on in the auditorium, I had no trouble picking out Jeremy McCormick's seat. Every seat in the house was clearly visible.

"Let me give you a quick geography lesson," Leah began. "You'll make your entrance from over there, in the right wing."

"And how do I get there in the first place?" I asked.

"Good question. There are stairs leading up to that side of the stage from the basement and a corridor that runs under us to the Green Room," she explained, tracing the journey with her finger from my entrance wing, across the stage and toward the left wing.

"Good to know," I said. "I had to do a show once on a platform that looked like a real stage, but it actually wasn't. The client wanted me to enter from the right side and the only way to pull it off was to pre-set me there before doors. And then I had to sit there, waiting ninety minutes until my introduction. So, from that night on, I always check ahead of time for a way on and a way off."

"Not a problem here, thankfully," Leah said with a laugh.

She picked up a portable headset from the coffee table in

front of the couch and pulled it on, flipping a switch on a small black box as she attached it to her belt.

"Kanisha, we're ready for the opening cue," she said into the headset. She nodded as she listened for a moment, then turned to me. "They're still writing a couple of light cues up in the booth," she said with a wave toward the back of the house.

On the back wall, about a half-story up, I could see a set of small windows. A silhouetted figure waved back.

We stood awkwardly on the stage, waiting for the lighting cue to get written. I glanced around at the set and a question occurred to me.

"During the show," I said as I moved toward the couch. "When Lloyd Williams' character is killed, he falls right about here, am I right?" I pointed to a spot on the stage directly behind the couch.

"I think that's about right," Leah agreed. "Why do you ask?"

I looked over at her. "I should warn you, I have—on occasion—become entwined in police investigations. So, I've gotten in the habit of trying to work things out in my head."

"Me too," Leah said as she moved toward me. "What are you thinking?"

"I'm just wondering, when the set went dark during the show, if it would be possible for Williams to crawl off stage, over to the right wing where I'll be entering from ..."

"... and then head downstairs, make his way through the corridor under the stage, run up the steps to the lobby, grab the knife and kill Jeremy McCormick?"

"And then get back here on-stage before the lights came back on?"

"I've had that same thought," Leah said. "He certainly might have had enough time. I don't know the exact running time of that scene; from my perspective it lasts forever. But he'd have to pass right through the Green Room, and I'm guessing Omar would have seen him. Plus, he'd also have to come up the stairs on the other side to get to the double blackout doors that go to the lobby. So, it's pretty likely Gloria and Tom would have spotted him as well."

"Yeah, Alex said he could see both of them in the wings," I added. I sat down on the couch and looked up at her. "So, you've been puzzling on this mystery as well?"

Leah sat down next to me, adjusting the black box on her belt as she did. "I've had my own experiences with police investigations since I got here, and after a couple of those it becomes hard not to turn yourself into a mini-Sherlock Holmes."

"So, you're new to the theater?"

"Well, I'm new to this theater," she said. "I acted in New York for a while and then, when this job came up, I decided it was time for a change."

"Were you familiar with the cast before you joined the show?"

Leah shook her head. "I'd done a couple shows with Alex since I arrived," she said. "And I'd seen Omar in a show. And Gloria, too, now that I think of it. But Lloyd Williams was new to me. And Tom Drake, I guess, is entirely new to theater."

I nodded and we sat in silence for several moments.

"Alex said both he and Williams had a bad history with the victim, Jeremy McCormick," I said, once again returning to the topic of the recent murder. "And Omar confirmed Gloria once had a fling with McCormick, but he wasn't sure how long ago it was or how it ended. Apparently, Gloria has a history of flings with cast members."

"You're not the first to mention it," Leah said. "I know her type. Seems like there's always one in every show."

"Omar said she appears to have broken that habit, though," I added. "At least, on this show."

I was about to continue on that thread when Leah suddenly held up one finger. She pressed the other hand against her earpiece. After a moment of listening, she nodded and turned to me.

"Kanisha's ready to run the opening," she said as she stood. "Why don't you take your place off-stage?"

I nodded and got up, heading toward the right wing. I turned back as Leah stepped off stage in the other direction. She spoke into her headset.

"Cue the opening."

From where I stood, I could see Leah clearly on the other side of the stage, standing in the wings. I realized that Alex had been correct: Gloria and Tom would have been easily visible while he was on-stage. Even if he was busy trying to murder Leah—or, actually, her character—at the time.

Suddenly, a loud drumroll blasted out of the speakers as moving lights began to ballyhoo the stage. A moment later, a pre-recorded announcer's voice echoed through the empty theater.

"Ladies and gentlemen, welcome to the 65th Annual Como Lake Players Preview Gala!"

Lively music replaced the drumroll, but the lights kept sweeping the stage.

"Please welcome tonight's host, magician extraordinaire ... Simon Hartwell!"

Leah yelled to me from her position across the stage. "Don't worry, we'll be re-recording that!"

I nodded as I stepped out onto the stage. The ballyhoo receded and the lights came up full.

"Good evening," I said to the dark and empty auditorium. I glanced at the script in my hands and then turned to Leah. "A quick technical question."

"That's why we call it a technical rehearsal," she said as she re-joined me center stage.

"If those steps are going to be here on show night, then I can bring people on stage for some tricks," I said as I gestured toward the temporary stair unit. "If not, then I can re-jigger the act so that no one needs to come on-stage."

"Let me check." She quickly relayed my question into her headset. She nodded as she listened, and then turned to me.

"Kanisha said we'll have a sturdier stair unit in place, but it will be stage left. That is, on our left, as we face the audience," she continued. "Oh, wait, sorry, you probably knew that already, didn't you? I mean, you're a professional," she said, quickly turning apologetic.

I nodded and smiled. "Not to worry. Years of corporate shows, with executives who never learned the difference between Stage Left and Stage Right, have reinforced the vital need for that refresher course."

I looked over at where the steps would be during the show. "I won't bring anyone up for this first segment. I'll just do something quick to establish my character. But when I do bring someone on stage, how tough is it to bring up the houselights a bit, so they can see where they're going?"

Before Leah could reply, the house lights quickly popped on in response.

"Apparently, it's no problem at all," she said. "Kanisha is very good." Something in her ear interrupted her and she listened quietly for a moment. "She wants a minute to write a quick house light cue, to have as a go-to for during the show."

"No problem," I said as I flipped through my script pages. I was thinking about adding in a rope trick for my second segment, now that I knew for sure I could bring someone up from the audience.

Leah headed back to her side of the stage to grab her clipboard. She listened at her headset for a moment and then turned to me. "We're going dark for a moment while she finesses this cue."

Before I could respond, the lights snapped off, plunging us into darkness.

One moment I'd been able to see Leah standing in the wings and then nothing at all, in any direction. A thought began to form in my mind and it came to the surface just as the lights returned.

"Can we do that again?" I asked as I moved toward the refrigerator at the rear of the set.

"Do what? Go dark?"

"If it's not a big problem," I said. "I just want to try something out."

Before Leah could even repeat the message, Kanisha had once again shut off all the lights. I reached out in the darkness and found the handle to the refrigerator door. I pulled it open and looked around the stage as the small amount of light spilled out.

"During the show—not the upcoming Gala, but during *Wait Until Dark*—is this how dark the room gets during that final blackout scene?"

"It sure is," Leah said, her voice coming out of the darkness.

"Interesting," I said slowly. After a moment, I realized we were all standing in the dark. "Thanks, you can bring the lights back on."

A moment later, the stage was once again flooded with light.

I squinted as I glanced down at the floor where Williams had been lying the night Megan and I saw the show. I looked over to where the steps were now—Stage Right—and then looked over at where they'd be during the Gala. I continued to scan the stage until I saw Leah, staring back at me from the wings.

"What is it?" she asked as she walked toward me. We met center stage.

"I think I just figured it out," I said slowly, afraid that uttering those simple words might make the idea vanish into the deep recesses of my brain.

But the more I thought about it, the more right it felt.

I thought about Williams counting—and miscounting—the cards that night at the bar and how Uncle Harry had railed against self-working tricks.

I thought about teaching Alex to be consistent with all of his moves while performing *Matrix*, in order to cover the sleights. And about how he'd unwittingly created a pattern and then, by breaking that pattern, drew attention to himself.

And I thought about the placement of the stair unit today, and where it would be the night of the Gala.

And I suddenly knew how and why Jeremy McCormick had been killed and—more importantly—who had done it.

I turned to Leah. "How close are you with the St. Paul Police Homicide Division?"

"Oddly enough, they're on my speed dial," she said. "What have you got?"

Once I said it out loud—and Leah added some thoughts of her own—we realized that calling the police was our best, next step.

The call took five minutes and then we continued with the technical rehearsal. But to be honest, I could tell our hearts weren't really in it anymore. We still had murder on our minds.

7

"THANKS FOR COMING EVERYONE."

This short welcome announcement was given in the flat, even voice of Detective Dietz as the invitees stood awkwardly near the stage. Although not a commanding figure, his years of experience somehow made him quickly the center of attention in a situation like this one.

And being a Homicide detective also didn't hurt.

"Some new information about the case has come to our

attention," he continued. "And rather than bring you all in one at a time, I thought it might be more efficient to do this as a group."

This invite-only presentation had definitely been his idea. Once Leah and I recounted our theory to him over the phone, he'd come to the theater and asked us to physically walk-through our scenario. At the conclusion of our demonstration, he'd sat quietly for several moments in the seat where Jeremy McCormick had died. His quiet demeanor reminded me of a Civics teacher I'd had back in high school who always remained calm and cool, regardless of the shenanigans taking place in his classroom.

"I think, given the lack of actual physical evidence, it would be more productive to bring the entire cast together for this," he finally said. "The individual personalities and group dynamics might work to our advantage."

And so, the cast had been given an early call time for their Thursday night performance of *Wait Until Dark*, arriving well before any of the ushers or other volunteer staff were on hand.

The only non-cast members present were me, Detective Dietz, and Gloria's husband. He looked just as sullen as he had the night I'd met him at the bar. After a grunted introduction, I learned his name was Sean.

"This is Eli Marks," Detective Dietz continued, nodding his head in my direction. "I've asked him to lead this short re-enactment, which I think we all might find illuminating." He stepped aside and gestured that the floor was now mine.

"Thanks, Detective," I said. "Leah and I have a theory about how and why Jeremy McCormick was murdered. To best explain our thinking, I'd like everyone to go to where you were when the crime occurred."

I turned quickly to Omar, who had started to head toward the exit. "Omar, we know you were downstairs in the Green

Room. For the purposes of this demonstration, why don't you just sit on that stair unit by the stage?"

He nodded in agreement while the rest of the cast moved up onto the set.

"I'm not really sure why I'm here," Sean said. He and Gloria had come in together, but as soon as she headed toward her spot in the wings, he immediately looked awkward and unhappy. Although, to be fair, he hadn't looked all that excited before that.

"Sean, you are here as a representative member of the audience," I explained. "Why don't you just take the seat you had that night, if you remember where it was."

He nodded and crossed the aisle to his seat, grumbling something I couldn't quite hear. I turned to Detective Dietz. "And why don't you take the hot seat, where Jeremy McCormick was sitting that night?"

The Detective moved to the back row and settled into the seat. We exchanged a look. I can't be entirely certain what it meant, but it felt like he was communicating *'Hey, stupid, don't screw this up.'* I tried to offer a return look which said, *'Not to worry. I've got this.'* However, I wasn't at all confident I'd expressed that sentiment, so instead I turned to the stage to see how the actors were doing getting into position.

Lloyd Williams was standing by the couch. Although normally pretty cocky, the sight of the Detective and the announcement of this re-enactment seemed to have taken some of the wind out of his sails. Alex and Leah were standing in front of the couch. Alex had just bent down and gingerly tipped the coffee table over, so it would be consistent with that moment in the play.

Seeing that Alex was going for that level of verisimilitude, Williams reluctantly lay down on the stage, taking the position his character falls into after being murdered. I could see his feet sticking out from behind the couch.

Gloria and Tom Drake had disappeared into the wings, although I could see Gloria peeking out from around the curtain.

"For the purposes of this demonstration," I said loudly so they could hear me from the back of the house, "why don't Gloria and Tom step on-stage just a bit, so you can see what's going on?"

They both stepped forward without enthusiasm.

"Kanisha, can you hear me?" I said as I turned toward the back wall of the theater. I could see just a trickle of light coming from the windows of the technical booth high up on the back wall.

"Loud and clear," came her muffled voice.

"Great. Let's go to lighting cue number one."

She must have been poised and ready for this instruction, for a moment later the lighting in the room changed dramatically. The stage lights went on full, while the house dimmed to what she had told me was "half." That is, not as dark as it was during the show, but just light enough so we could see what was going on in the house.

"Okay, for our purposes, let's pretend this lighting represents how things looked before the black-out. Then we'll switch to our modified 'black-out' look," I requested.

A second later, the white lights on stage went out, leaving only a spooky blue glow covering the stage.

"For our demonstration, this represents the black-out look," I said as I turned toward the auditorium's entrance doors. Detective Dietz gave me the slightest of nods from his seat, while on the other side of the aisle, Gloria's husband glared at me. The reflected blue light from the stage gave his already sunken eyes a menacing tinge.

As I reached the doors, I turned and addressed the cast on-stage.

"Once the black-out occurred, the clock was ticking for our

killer. They had to leave their current position, make their way to the lobby, and grab the knife which lay next to the Opening Night cake."

I dramatically pulled a butter knife from my jacket pocket; I'd picked it up earlier in the theater's small kitchenette.

"Then, as quietly as possible, the killer had to move through first the outer door to the auditorium ... wait for that door to close completely ... and then move through the inner door, ensuring that no light leaks would give them away."

I stepped out of the auditorium for what I hoped was a dramatic moment, and then re-entered through the second door. I stood for a moment at the top of the center aisle.

"Time is running out and I have to be quick," I continued. "It's dark, but I know where my victim is sitting: On the left, four seats in. Feeling for the seats, I ease my way down the back wall until I count the fourth seat. I stab the victim repeatedly in the back, at the very moment that everyone in the audience is jumping at Alex's back-from-the-dead attack on Leah. The audience's screams cover up any sounds the victim might make. Assured my work is complete, I leave the knife in his back. I feel my way to the entrance door, slip through it, waiting until it is completely closed. And then I move back into the lobby. Mission accomplished."

I looked down the long aisle toward the cast assembled on-stage. They stared back at me for a long moment.

"That's nice and all," Omar finally said from his position on the stairs. "But how is that new? I mean, isn't that what happened?"

"It is what happened," I said. "But I don't think that's what was *supposed* to happen."

I moved back to my position directly in front of the closed doors.

"I think the direction our killer received was this: 'The victim's on the left. The fourth seat.'"

From my position in front of the doors, I turned slightly to my left and indicated Detective Dietz, who sat four seats in from the aisle.

"The problem, as it turns out, was that the person offering that plan meant *stage left*," I continued. "Which, from this new perspective facing the stage, is actually on my right. So, in reality, the killer should have turned *right*, counted four seats, and stabbed *that* person."

I matched my actions to my words and found myself on the opposite side of the back row. The person sitting in the seat in front of me was Gloria's husband, Sean.

"It was simple, really," I continued. "People get this mixed up all the time. The difference between audience left and stage left. Especially people who are new to the theater."

This last statement had its intended effect. Tom Drake pushed himself away from Gloria, pointing a shaking finger at her as he stumbled toward center stage.

"It was all her idea," he yelped. "She planned it, she made me do it."

"What are you saying?" Gloria screamed back. "I had no idea you were planning such a thing. I love my husband." She turned toward Detective Dietz, who had crossed the aisle to stand next to me. "Don't listen to anything he says. He's lying, I swear he's lying."

"She set the whole thing up," Tom Drake continued. It looked like he was hyper-ventilating. "She pointed her husband out from backstage. 'There he is,' she said. 'On the left. Fourth seat.' I got through the doors and I did what she said. Fourth seat on the left."

"You're an idiot," Gloria shot back and leapt toward him. Two uniformed cops appeared suddenly from the other wing and stepped between the couple, pulling them apart and quickly snapping handcuffs on the pair.

"Well, we can sort all that out downtown," Dietz said

slowly. He sauntered down the aisle and looked up at Leah. "I'm afraid you're going to be a couple actors short this weekend."

"That's okay," she said. "It's kind of a badge of honor to close a show early when it's selling out. Plus, that will give us a head start on installing the set for the next show, which is already selling quite nicely."

"I know," he said. "My wife has already bought tickets." I couldn't tell from his tone if this was a good thing or not.

I watched as the two cops escorted Gloria and Tom up the center aisle. Her husband simply glared at her as she was marched past. The couple were still trading barbs after they disappeared through the double doors, their voices echoing out in the lobby. After several moments, all was quiet.

"How did you know she was having an affair with Tom?" This came from Alex. He and Williams had stepped to the edge of the stage to watch the couple's exit.

"It's just like that move in *Matrix* we were talking about," I said. "Gloria had established a pattern—always having a fling with a cast member—and then drew attention to herself when she broke that pattern. I imagine once she hatched her plan with Tom Drake, they went to great lengths to cover any hint that they were involved. If there was no evidence of involvement between them, I think she felt that could create a stronger alibi for them during the murder."

"She knew I could see them in the wings before the blackout," Alex said. "And that I'd assume Tom was still there in the dark."

"If nothing else, I think this points out the dangers of show romances," Omar suddenly offered from his position on the stairs.

Although I don't think the others noticed it, I'm sure I detected a quick look between Alex and Leah.

"I actually think they knew each other from outside the

theater," Leah said quickly. "Doing the show together was just part of her larger plan."

"Yes, yes, well it will all be sorted out in the wash," Dietz said to no one in particular. "The best laid plans ..."

"It's like what your uncle Harry said about self-working tricks," Alex said, with a quick glance over at Williams. "They're not self-working if you can't even count properly."

I don't think his fellow actor caught the subtle dig.

"Yes, like Harry said, a truly self-working trick is something of a unicorn in the magic world," I agreed.

"Anyway," Detective Dietz said, clearly not interested in the mechanics of magic tricks. "I'm sure we'll need you two to come down at some point and make an official statement."

He nodded first at me and then at Leah.

"No problem," she said.

"Absolutely," I said.

He looked at us for a long moment, turning from me to Leah and then back to me. "You know, I made some calls about you," he said. He was barely suppressing a smile. Something seemed to be striking him funny, although it wasn't clear what it might be. I felt like it might be me. "You seem to have something of a reputation with the Homicide folks in Minneapolis," he continued.

"I suppose that's possible," I agreed.

"And this one," he said, turning back to Leah. "This one is already developing a reputation of her own over here in St. Paul."

"Sadly, that is true," Leah said, not even bothering to suppress a grin.

Detective Dietz gave us another long look as he headed toward the exit. "Well, in future, I would suggest you two stick to your respective occupations in your corresponding cities."

Leah shrugged. "Never say never."

I smiled at her. "That's right. Never say never."

GET YOUR FREE COMO LAKE PLAYERS SHORT MYSTERY

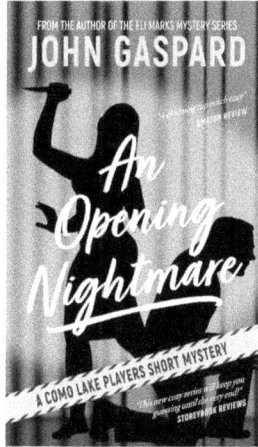

An Opening Nightmare

A Como Lake Players Short Mystery

A Killer Show, With the Corpses To Prove It

When an audience member is stabbed in the middle of an Opening Night performance, Leah must figure out who this clever killer is ... and make sure they don't kill the run of her show! Or murder her, as well!

A great introduction to The Como Lake Players mystery series: New Executive Director (and former actress) Leah Sexton must navigate the twisty world of community theater while dealing with crazy Board members, egomaniacal directors, self-centered actors ... and the occasional cold-blooded killer.

"This new cozy series will keep you guessing until the very end!" — Storeybook Reviews

https://www.albertsbridgebooks.com

ACTING CAN BE MURDER

A COMO LAKE PLAYERS MYSTERY (BOOK ONE)

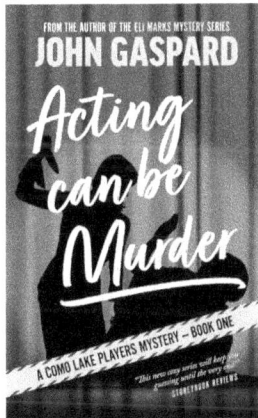

The Phrase "Dying On Stage"
Takes on a Whole New Meaning

After fleeing a failed relationship in New York, actress Leah Sexton finds herself as the new Executive Director of the Como Lake Players–a small community theater nestled in a sleepy St. Paul neighborhood. The initial calm of this new position is shattered immediately when a local critic–who had just panned the theater's latest production–is found murdered on the show's set.

On the heels of this grisly discovery, the show's lead actress tumbles down a flight of stairs–or was she pushed? In order to keep the show running and the theater afloat, Leah offers to step into the leading role. The arrival of her ex-boyfriend amid anonymous threats against her and the show require Leah to act as if her life depends on it. Because it does.

(Previously released under the pen name Bobbie Raymond)

Grab this funny, twisty mystery today!
https://www.albertsbridgebooks.com

JOIN THE NEWSLETTER

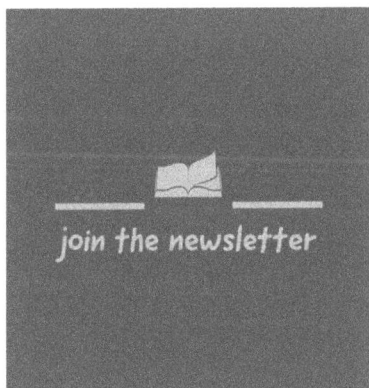

Keep in touch about all the books at Albert's Bridge books —
The Como Lake Players mysteries ... the Eli Marks mysteries ...
plus occasional deals on other mysteries! And no spam!

Go to: https://www.elimarksmysteries.com

THE SWORD & MR. STONE

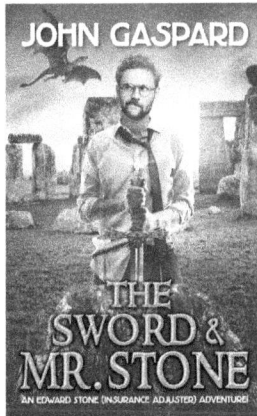

A Wild Modern-Day Quest for King Arthur's Magical Sword, Excalibur!

Insurance adjuster Edward Stone's quiet life is completely upset when he's drawn into a wild search for King Arthur's fabled lost sword, Excalibur.

From the towering monuments of Stonehenge to the dark mists of Loch Ness, Stone finds himself battling evil forces intent upon possessing this long-lost treasure.

It's only when he embraces the magical nature of the legend that's Stone is finally able to harness the epic forces behind Excalibur, the Sword of Power.

"A hero is no braver than an ordinary man, but he is brave five minutes longer." — Ralph Waldo Emerson

Grab this funny, gripping adventure today!
https://www.albertsbridgebooks.com

THE GREYHOUND OF THE BASKERVILLES

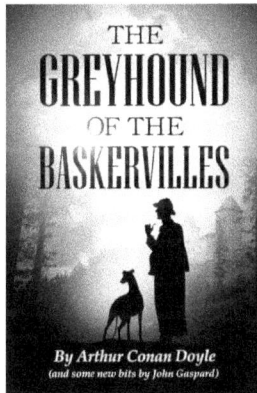

A new take on the Arthur Conan Doyle's classic mystery, "The Hound of the Baskervilles."

Think you know this story? Well, you haven't experienced it until you've read it through the eyes of Sherlock's pet dog.

It's the classic tale, now narrated by a dog. A greyhound, in fact, named Septimus.

Holmes and Watson ... and Septimus ... are called to the
Baskerville estate to protect the new Baron and see if there is
any truth to the legend of the hound of the Baskervilles. It's a
dog-meet-dog mystery as Septimus sniffs out the clues, detects
the red herrings and goes head-to-head with the monsterous
creature which is haunting the moors.
It's the classic you love ... but now it's a slightly different tail!

"A delightful tale, familiar and yet filled with surprises."

Grab it now!
★★★★★
https://www.albertsbridgebooks.com

THE RIPPEROLOGISTS

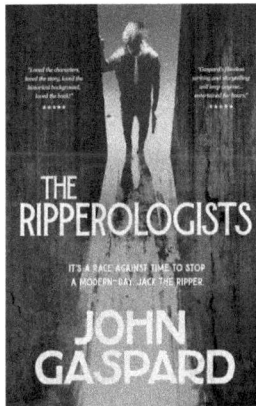

"Who are you?"

"For tonight, you can call me Jack. Mind if I come in?"

"Fascinating, couldn't put it down!"
Nunes, Amazon.com (verified purchase)
★★★★★

When a copycat serial killer begins recreating Jack the Ripper's 1888 murder spree, two competing experts are forced to work together to stop him.

What they don't understand is that his murderous spree is far more personal than either of them ever suspected.

Grab this electrifying race-against-time mystery/thriller today!

https://www.albertsbridgebooks.com

★ ★ ★ ★ ★

LISTEN TO THE PODCAST

Listen to the audiobook versions of the Eli Marks mysteries ... for FREE. And learn more about the lives of magicians and performers and other ideas found in the Eli Marks series.

Each episode includes interviews with guest experts and magicians ... plus a reading of a chapter from an Eli Marks mystery. Season One presents great guests (like Dick Cavett and The Amazing Kreskin) and a full reading of the first book in the series, "The Ambitious Card."

Season Two provides a free reading of the second book in the series, "The Bullet Catch," plus great interviews.

Go to: https://www.elimarksmysteries.com

BOOKS BY JOHN GASPARD

The Como Lake Players Mysteries
ACTING CAN BE MURDER
DYING TO AUDITION
REHEARSED TO DEATH

The Eli Marks Mystery Series
THE AMBITIOUS CARD (#1)
THE BULLET CATCH (#2)
THE MISER'S DREAM (#3)
THE LINKING RINGS (#4)
THE FLOATING LIGHT BULB (#5)
THE ZOMBIE BALL (#6)
THE MAGIC SQUARE (#7)
THE SELF-WORKING TRICK (#8)

Stand-Alone Novels
THE SWORD & MR. STONE
A CHRISTMAS CARL
THE GREYHOUND OF THE BASKERVILLES
THE RIPPEROLOGISTS

<u>Filmmaking Books</u>
FAST, CHEAP AND UNDER CONTROL
FAST, CHEAP AND WRITTEN THAT WAY
TELL THEM IT'S A DREAM SEQUENCE
WOMEN MAKE MOVIES

ABOUT THE AUTHOR

John is author of the Eli Marks mystery series as well as four other stand-alone novels, *"The Sword & Mr. Stone," "A Christmas Carl," "The Greyhound of the Baskervilles"* and *"The Ripperologists."*

He also writes the *Como Lake Players* mystery series.

In real life, John's not a magician, but he has directed six low-budget features that cost very little and made even less—that's no small trick.

He's also written books on the subject of low-budget film-making. Ironically, they've made more than the films. Those books (*"Fast, Cheap and Under Control"* and *"Fast, Cheap and Written That Way"*) are available in eBook, Paperback and audiobook formats.

John lives in Minnesota and shares his home with his lovely wife, several dogs, a few cats and a handful of pet allergies.

Find out more at: https://www.albertsbridgebooks.com and https://www.elimarksmysteries.com.

facebook.com/JohnGaspardAuthorPage

twitter.com/johngaspard

instagram.com/johngaspard

bookbub.com/authors/john-gaspard

www.ingramcontent.com/pod-product-compliance
Lightning Source LLC
Chambersburg PA
CBHW062123020426
42335CB00013B/1075